TALKING ROUND THE CALENDAR

TALKING ROUND
THE CALENDAR

*Addresses to Children
and Young People*

by

CYRIL DAVEY

LUTTERWORTH PRESS
LONDON

*This book has been printed in Great Britain by
litho-offset at Taylor Garnett Evans & Co. Ltd.,
Watford, Herts, and bound by them*

Cynical Comment

by

A Distinguished Preacher

*" The ideal children's
address deals with
kindness to grandma
and the cat . . .
especially the cat ! "*

These talks
are offered to those
who believe in kindness but
who believe, too, that God
gave preachers ten minutes
of the morning service
to use for better
things.

CONTENTS

8 CONTENTS

AUTHOR'S FOREWORD

THERE was once a builder's foreman who is reputed to have said that he liked children in the abstract but detested them in the concrete. Not a few preachers would agree with him. They will usually find it hard to talk to children in morning service or club because they cannot even begin to poke their heads into a child's mind. Nobody, however childlike a genius he may be, can get inside their minds completely, but whoever would talk to or write for children cannot entirely neglect this exercise.

It needs to be practised—outside the pulpit, and probably most usefully when the children are in their dressing-gowns or their baths.

There is no technique which can be taught from books. The first lesson, if a book could teach anything at all, would begin thus: "You must, of course, like children—in the concrete." If, because you like them, you begin to tell them a story, one or two principles will quickly become evident.

They don't like being talked-down-to.

They don't like pauses, either vocal or narrative. In the bath they will begin to look for the soap and in church for their collection.

They don't like rhetorical questions. The preacher who indulges in them is asking for awkward shocks. On the other hand, they enjoy being allowed to help the speaker to develop his talk. In those talks which follow will be found some indications of this question-and-answer method, though it is not always applicable. There is no irreverence in a to-and-fro traffic between pulpit and children's pews, though it may sometimes lead a congregation to wish they had the same liberty. Indeed, as some preachers have already found, it might lead a congregation nearer to understanding what we're getting at than . . . But that is another subject!

Lastly, to come back to the children, they do like to know "Why?"

"Why Advent?" "Why Remembrance Day?" "Why Ascension Day?"

It was to answer such essential questions as these last ones that these talks were first given.

It only remains to be added that, just as no man can preach another man's sermon with conviction, so no one can give someone else's children's address. It must be taken, twisted, transformed and made one's own. Or, to change the metaphor, the skeleton which the writer provides must be clothed with flesh by the speaker—and, in different hands, the bare bones will be very differently clad.

Several of these addresses have appeared in shorter form in the British Weekly, *and I must gratefully acknowledge the editor's permission to use them here.*

Advent

QUEER CALENDARS

WHAT are calendars for?
They tell us what day it is, of course,
and something else.

What month it is, and probably which year.
And you don't need to be very clever to know
how many months there are on every calendar.

But has every calendar got twelve months on it?

You would think it expensive and a bit silly to
send someone a calendar which had only one
month. And sillier still to send a calendar that
had only twenty-four days marked on it, and not
even the name of the month!

It was just that kind of calendar which came to
our house once. It seemed like an early Christmas
present, since it was brightly coloured, except that
it came at the end of November. In a way, it *was*.
At least, it was an Advent present. It came to us
from Germany, and if you lived in that country,
or one of a number of other countries in Europe,
you would know what it was straight away, for
you would find them in the shops and in people's
houses everywhere. They are not all exactly like
the one we have at home, of course, but if I tell
you how that one works you will see what it is
all about.

It is really just a picture, you think. At the bottom is old Santa Claus, dragging a sleigh and carrying a sack on his shoulder. He has stopped for a minute or two to unload a great heap of parcels from his bag. From the ground a ladder leads up to the sky, leaning on a big patch of fleecy cloud. A laughing man-in-the-moon beams down on half a dozen little cherubs who are carrying parcels up the ladder towards the cloud. In the cloud is a large wooden door, with an angel poking his head out of a window in the cloud to see who is ringing the door-bell.

Now the queerest thing about the calendar is that each of these parcels is really a little door in the cardboard calendar. You can open them one by one and find what is in the parcel, because behind it is a picture. In one there is a doll, in another a toy engine, and in others an apple, a gingerbread man, a wooden sledge and so on.

Every one of the little doors has a number on it, going up from "1" at the bottom to "23" on the parcel in the little angel's hand by the wooden door.

What do you think it is all about?

The weeks before Christmas are called Advent. You know what that word means? "Coming." And you know whose coming we are thinking about at this time of the year? At least, we *ought* to be thinking about it, though we *may* be thinking of parties and presents most of the time. All December, until Christmas, is the Advent season.

How many days are there between the beginning of December and Christmas Day? Twenty-four.

On every one of those days, probably before they go to school, children all over Germany will open one of the little doors to see what is behind it. But do you remember what the number was on the parcel by the door? "23", not "24".

And that only takes us up to the day before Christmas Eve. Where do you think the last number is?

On the big wooden door itself. So that on Christmas Eve the door is opened and inside we see . . . can you guess what?

A lovely little picture of Mary, with the baby Jesus in her arms.

Every one of the parcels is a present left for Him. Every morning is one day nearer to the day when the door is opened and we shall see Him. Every day in Advent is a day nearer to the great and wonderful day when we remember that Jesus came into our world as a little child.

CHRISTMAS ALGEBRA

Isn't it nice to be on holiday, especially at Christmas, and forget all about school? Particularly if you are in the forms which are struggling with French and Geometry and Chemical Equations and Algebra.

But it is not a good thing to get out of practice, so we are going to start off this Christmas talk with a bit of . . . what do you think? A bit of algebra!

If you are feeling put off by that idea let's try and find out something else first. Think of the word "Christmas". What does the "mas" part of it mean?

Probably the nearest we shall get to it is "feast" or "festival". So that "Christmas" ought to mean . . .? The Festival of Christ. There are many times in the life of Jesus when we would hardly think it was right to have parties and sing cheerful songs and look as gay as we can. It certainly would not be right on Palm Sunday, or Good Friday. But at Christmas we can't help being gay. There is the best reason in the world for being happy.

But this is just where the Algebra comes in.

There was once a school-master who was

14

teaching the third form, who had just begun to learn the subject for the first time. He could never seem to understand why they found it puzzling. He would walk up and down the classroom until he found a boy with a look of misery on his face and then thunder out: "Come here, boy! Out to the blackboard! What's the matter? Nothing difficult about it! All you need to do is find the answer—and you know what that is already! Put it down!" When the poor boy looked more upset than ever, he would bang the blackboard. "Write it down, boy! *X*! That's the answer! *X*! Don't you know what 'x' means? The unknown quantity! *X is the unknown quantity!* Now go back and work it out!" So the terrified boy would go back to his desk and try to remember that if you know "x is the unknown quantity" you can easily find the answer.

It isn't so easy as that, of course—even if it sounds easy, which it doesn't.

But remember what the teacher said. "X is the unknown."

Now think of shop-windows and Christmas cards and advertisements in the papers. What do they say is coming? Christmas? They don't, you know—at least, not always. They often shorten it to something else.

"X-mas." Yes. And you remember what the teacher said that "X" meant.

What *ought* to be the "Festival of Jesus" is to many people "the festival of the unknown".

How many people will remember that it *is* the feast of joy for Jesus' birth? Some people, but not everyone.

In some parts of Austria they used to put a chair at the head of the table on Christmas Day, where no one was allowed to sit. It was the chair where Jesus would have been sitting if He had come into the house while they were celebrating His own feast. It might not be a bad idea if we did the same thing. It would remind us that we are not only right to be gay and happy, but that we have the best reason in the world for it.

DEMON-KINGS AND FAIRIES

T<small>HERE</small> can't be any boy or girl who has never been to a pantomime, surely?

Pantomimes are one of the queerest things about the English Christmas, and no visitor to Britain can really understand what they are all about. That is not surprising. You go to see the Babes in the Wood—and you find it all mixed up with Robin Hood and his Merry Men. You go to see Cinderella—and find the two ugly sisters are really funny men. You go to see Dick Whittington—and find that he is a girl. Robinson Crusoe has Chinese acrobats doing juggling on the docks. Jack and the Beanstalk has a comic cow which is never far away. And everybody in the audience joins in the songs. Is it any wonder a stranger from Europe or America can't understand pantomimes?

The pantomime idea is nearly three hundred years old in this country, and there have been a great many changes in it. Our grandfathers always used to look forward to the clown with a string of sausages and the comic policeman. *We* never see them. But one thing has not altered very much.

The show may begin with village lads and

lasses on the green singing a chorus, or the funny men riding hobby horses after the hounds. But very soon we begin the story itself. It has usually hardly begun before the "bad man" appears. You know at once who he is, for the lights go down a little and perhaps a green spotlight is thrown on him. Sometimes the very thing happens which our fathers used to see.

The stage grows dark. Then, from the left-hand side of the stage as you look at it, there comes on the Demon-King. Everyone used to shiver in their shoes, for he would look very fierce and evil. The small children would put their faces in their hands and say: "Tell me when he's gone. I don't like him."

You know what the Demon-King would have to say—the same as the bad man still says in *our* show. "*I'll* put a stop to Cinderella marrying the Prince—or Dick getting to London and becoming Lord Mayor. I'll have him killed . . . or sent to a desert island. The plot is going to work out all wrong. And the hero shan't win after all."

Then, when everyone was feeling how dreadful it was going to be, there was a movement on the other side of the stage and there, in a circle of white light, stood . . .

Yes, the Good Fairy. "Go!" she said, waving her wand. "You have no power while I'm around. Jack shall have his Jill and all shall be well."

All through the pantomime which follows there

is a struggle between the Good Fairy and the Demon-King. Sometimes we tremble in our seats because the wrong side seems to be winning. When that happens there are good reasons for it. The hero has forgotten the good advice the fairy gave him. Or he has been disobedient. Or perhaps he has decided that he can manage very well by himself, without any help from the Good Fairy. Then everything goes wrong. But somehow the fairy is always at hand to put things right if the hero will only turn back, or listen to what she says.

Have you ever thought that a pantomime is just like life, and we are just like the hero?

There is a fight going on all through our own lives between good and evil. Of course you don't believe in fairies—but we *do* believe in something much more important. We believe in God. God wants us to win in this fight between the good and the bad. We *can* win, too. But the times when we lose the fight are the same in real life as in the pantomime.

We want our own way. We think we can manage without God's help. We forget all about Him. And then, don't you think, we deserve to lose our fight with the devil?

But God is always there, even if we don't always see Him, and always ready to help us to start out again—with Him, and in His strength.

Epiphany

THREE WISE MEN FROM PERSIA

How many Wise Men were there?

You won't find anywhere in the Bible that there were three, although wherever you see them painted by the great artists, or even on Christmas cards, you will find three of them. Look it up when you go home and see if you can find anything about "three Wise Men".

By the way, which Gospel will you turn to, to find the story?

It is only in St. Matthew that we have the old story. On that very slender foundation, however, all kinds of legends have been built. You can probably think of some for yourselves. In some of the legends the Wise Men are kings; in some they come from different countries; in others, they have some very strange adventures on the way to Bethlehem. In most of the tales which have been told through the years, they are regarded as astronomers, with a great knowledge of the stars and their movements. Perhaps that is natural when we think of the star which guided them.

There is a Persian legend about them which can't possibly be true, but which has a very real truth hidden away in it.

They were not all old men, it says, and they

20

were certainly not kings. Indeed, if you had seen
them trotting across the desert on their camels
you might have been surprised at the differences
between them.

The first was a very old man, who seemed to
know all there was to know. His two companions
always spoke to him with the respect due to his
age and his wisdom. The second rode like a
soldier and, when he dismounted, and walked
around their little camp at night, he had the firm
step of a soldier. Wise man though he was, he
was a warrior too, in the middle years of his life.
The third was no more than a boy. It is true that
he was clever—and the son of a great and wise
man—but it was surprising to find him travelling
hundreds of miles across the desert to seek for
the king.

Where they would find the king whose birth
the star had announced, they had no idea, and,
though they were prepared for almost anything,
they were greatly astonished when they found
him in a stable. It was so small a stable that
there was room for only one of them at a time.
For a little while they discussed who should go
first to take his gift, for with all their wisdom and
power and cleverness they were very humble folk.

At last the old man was persuaded to enter.
The others waited outside, and they had to wait a
long time before he came back. When he did so,
at last, he looked surprised and very happy.

The soldier stayed longer still, and when he

returned he marched straight past them, walking to and fro under the stars, with his head high and his shoulders back.

The boy stayed longest of all, and when he came from the stable he was laughing.

They said nothing to each other and it seemed as though they wanted time to think about what they had seen. But at last the boy spoke.

"Wasn't it strange," he said, "that the king should be a boy of my own age?"

"Nonsense," said the soldier. "He was a man. You saw the wrong person."

"Of course he wasn't," laughed the boy. "We talked about the things boys think of—our hopes, what we are going to do in the world, how to make the best of our lives."

"I'm afraid somebody's been having a joke at your expense, my lad. The king was a soldier, I tell you. As he talked to me I saw, as I'd never seen before, how the whole of life is soldiering—fighting against evil and wrongdoing and temptation."

"He was a boy!" muttered the other.

The soldier turned to the wise old man. "Which of us is right? *You* can tell us."

The old man seemed to come out of a dream. "Neither of you is right. The man I saw was as old as I am—and wiser, much wiser." He paused for a moment. "We have seen a mystery this night. We have seen that God meets us all as we are."

Spring

THE VILLAGE OF FROZEN MUSIC

OLD Peter was a fiddler. Or so, at least, the Norwegian legend tells us.

You could not really have called him a violinist. It was much too grand a word for an old man who had spent all his life wandering from village to village, through the forests and across the mountains, with his violin under his arm, playing for his supper and his bed.

Everyone knew him, and nearly everyone loved him, though there were some who thought he should have done something more like "real work" than playing his fiddle. He would have answered that there was nothing better to do. He saw the country in all its moods, and brought pleasure to those who listened.

He wanted little enough. Enough money to buy a little food, and that he could usually get after he had played on the village green. And a bed for the night, with some supper if he were lucky. That was easy enough, too, as a rule. In the village inn he would sit and draw the old folk-tunes and dances from his fiddle. He brought custom to the inn, happiness to those who sat and talked by the fireside—and for that the landlord would gladly give him something to eat and a night's lodging on the straw.

Old Peter had known bad times, of course, but he had never been either starving or without shelter in some barn or hut, unless it was in the summer when he was happy to sleep under the trees. Then, at last, there came the winter when everything changed. The summer had been poor and the harvest had failed. Winter set in early and with it came a dreadful sickness which swept through the countryside. People who had not had enough to eat sickened quickly, and many died long before Christmas brought the turn of the year.

For the fiddler there was nothing. No one had time for him. No one wanted to listen to his gay music, and no one had either money or food to spare. He trudged helplessly on from village to village, until he felt that his old legs could carry him no further than the village which lay just ahead, where the spire of the little church peeped through the bare trees.

But there, too, none wanted him. The houses had closed doors and even the inn was empty. Peter made his way to the parsonage to ask for shelter. There was no room, said the pastor, standing in the doorway. The parsonage was full of sick people, and what food there was must be saved for them.

"You can sleep in the church," said the pastor. "It's cold, and the floor is hard, of course, but it will be a shelter from the wind."

As dusk fell people moved through the village and listened outside the door of the church. Peter was playing inside—not hymns, but the gay, sprightly dances of spring, the spring that seemed to be so far away. As the cold sharpened the listeners moved away and, after a while, the fiddler faltered in his playing, as though his fingers were too cold to hold the strings. The music stopped.

In the morning, when the pastor went across to the church, it was empty. He was surprised. It was not like Peter to go without saying farewell and thanks, even for such rough hospitality. But, as he moved down the church, the pastor saw why the fiddler had not said farewell. He had played his last dance. He lay, frozen in the cold night, with the fiddle clutched in his dead hand.

As the weeks went by the village forgot old Peter. The signs of spring were in the air. Here and there flowers began to peep and, in the rivers, the ice started to crack.

One morning a little girl passing the church heard a sound and ran to fetch her mother. Other people gathered quickly. From the church came the sound of music—the very dances old Peter had played on the last night of his life. They sprang, gay and sparkling, from the windows and the very walls themselves. The pastor came hurrying across to them, paused to listen, and opened the door.

"Peter!" he called.

The church was empty, though the music went on. It had been frozen into the walls on that bitter night. The spring thawed it out once more.

Sunshine, warmth, friendliness can bring frozen music out of many a cold heart.

H.

WHAT IS A CARNIVAL?

How many of you have seen a Carnival? What is it?

A procession, most people would say, with decorated wagons, and a queen with two or three attendants, and prizes for the best-dressed boys and girls. Usually they are held to raise money— sometimes for hospitals, sometimes for the local football club, sometimes for a whole lot of good causes. If you were to go to France or Switzerland or Italy, you would find carnivals that are much gayer than any you have seen in this country. You may have seen films of them. There are huge wagons, beautifully decorated; men on stilts, or wearing masks or heads as big as themselves; a band, of course, or even two or three bands. One of the most famous carnivals is called the "Battle of Flowers", where flowers are thrown from girls on the lorries to the people in the streets, and by the people in the streets to those who are passing by. Usually these carnivals end with a gay dance, not just in a public building, but in the open air. You would probably find hundreds and hundreds of people dancing in the streets and the squares, while a bright moon shone down in the warm half-tropical night.

That would be a Carnival worth seeing, wouldn't it?

But how did they first begin, and why were they called "carnivals"?

The word comes from two Latin words—*carnis* and *vale*. *Carnis* means . . .? Do you know what a "carnivorous animal" is? One which eats flesh, like a lion or a tiger. So *carnis* means "flesh". *Vale* is the Latin word for "farewell".

Carnival means: "farewell to the flesh".

This is how it came about. In the Middle Ages, when most Christians in Europe belonged to the Roman Catholic Church, everyone had to "fast" for forty days before Easter. You know what fasting is? Not giving up eating altogether, of course, but at any rate not eating meat, or flesh. The idea was that as each day came and men felt hungry they would say to themselves: "Why can't I have what I want to eat?" Then they would remember Jesus, and all He suffered for them.

That is a very sound idea. The forty days before Easter prepare us for Good Friday and Easter Sunday, just as Advent prepares us for Christmas.

Then people spoilt it. They said: "If we're going to give up eating flesh and meat, and if we're going to make our bodies suffer for six weeks—let's have a really good feast before we begin! Let's have a day when we can let ourselves go and do what we like!" So they did.

Just before the six weeks began they had a
holiday, eating and drinking to the full. They
called it the "Day of Carnival"—the day of
farewell to the flesh.

You know what those forty days are called by
the Church? Lent. And even in the middle of
Lent there were folk who had to take a day off
fasting and have a feast to get them through the
long weeks of discipline.

It wasn't a very good idea, really, was it?
Because it meant that they didn't want to fast at
all—and perhaps they didn't want to think about
Jesus and what He had suffered for them. It
doesn't sound as though some of them were very
sincere, if they had to have a feast first—and
probably another one when it was ended, as well
as a break in the middle.

One of the old prophets had something to say
to the Jews about this kind of thing. You will find
his words in the 6th chapter of Isaiah. He
makes God say: "I don't want you to fast, or give
things up, or even pretend to worship me unless
you mean it." The important thing we have to
think of at the beginning of Lent is *sincerity*.

Giving things up is silly—unless it helps us to
think of Jesus, and of all that He gave up for *us*.

Mother's Day

THE ARCHBISHOP AND THE SADHU

THE Archbishop of Canterbury looked very important, with his clerical collar, his black suit, his gaiters and his great silver cross hanging on a silver chain round his neck. The man who sat opposite to him in his study didn't seem to fit into the scene at all. He was tall, with a dark skin and a black beard, and his dress was a long, yellow robe which reached to his feet. On his head he wore a yellow turban. One look at him, and you would have known he was an Indian.

He was just saying something to the Archbishop.

"If I don't find my mother in heaven, I shall ask God to send me to hell so that I may be with her."

Fancy saying that to an archbishop!

The man in the yellow robe was one of the greatest Christians of this century. His name was Sundar Singh, and the yellow robe which he wore told everyone in India, at a glance, that he was a *sadhu*. That word means a "holy man"; not the kind of holy man who sits in the forest or the hills doing nothing, but one who tramps from village to village, talking and teaching. There were very few Christian *sadhus* in the East. Most of them were Hindus, and some were not good men at all, but men who only pretended to be good so that they could beg food and money.

Sundar Singh had not always been a Christian, either. Indeed, he didn't become one until he was fourteen years old. The story of his conversion is a very wonderful one, but it cannot be told here. You can read it for yourself. He was brought up in North India, in a village called Rampur, and by religion he was a Sikh. The Sikhs don't worship idols; they have a sacred book, just as we have our Bible; and the women, perhaps more than the men, love going to their churches, which are called *gurdwaras*.

Sundar used to go to worship with his mother from the days when she carried him on her hip. When he was old enough he began to learn the prayers which she said every day, and soon afterwards he started to learn his sacred book by heart. (How much of the Bible do *you* know by heart?)

Every week he used to trudge across the yellow, sandy desert with his mother to a little strip of forest. This was the great moment of the week, for in the forest lived a very old *sadhu*. Usually he said nothing at all to Sundar, though he sometimes would listen to the newest chapters he had learned. Sundar's mother knew nothing about Jesus—or almost nothing, for there were very few Christians in the village where they lived.

Certainly she wasn't a Christian, or anything like it.

When he was fourteen Sundar's mother died and it was only after that, by what seemed like a miracle, that he himself was converted and became a Christian.

In the years that followed he travelled all over India; went to Ceylon, Burma, China, Europe and America; and had the most astonishing adventures. He was beaten, stoned, imprisoned, and often left to die in the jungle or some worse place. He faced madmen and wild animals without any fears, and year after year crossed the towering Himalayas, tramping over the snow, and crawling across tree-trunks or ice-bridges over precipices, to reach the forbidden land of Tibet. Everything he suffered was because he loved Jesus and preached about Him wherever he went.

And yet his mother wasn't a Christian, nor his father, nor any of his boyhood friends.

But Sundar always said that he owed everything he was to his mother. She taught him to pray, and to love good things; to read the holy books of his own religion, and to be kind, honest and gentle. He didn't believe that God could possibly punish someone for not worshipping Him in the Christian way, if she had had no chance of knowing about Jesus. None of us believe that, either.

This is Mother's Day. Perhaps you've given

her some flowers already to say "Thank you" for all she does for you. Will you do something more? Every mother, like Sundar's own mother, wants her boy or girl to grow up to love the best, to serve God and to be good. The best thanks your Mother can have is to see you, like Sundar Singh, growing up to be the best she has ever dreamed for you.

B

_ H.

Palm Sunday

THE DONKEY AND THE ROBIN

WHAT has a donkey got on his back?
Next time you see one in a field—but
perhaps you had better not go too close unless
he looks very tame! Have a look at the donkeys
on the beach next time you are on the sands.

From their neck almost down to their tails
runs a dark line. Across their back, down to the
tops of their front legs, runs another dark line.

If you try to draw those lines, what shape do
they make? A cross. And the quick-thinking
ones know already why the donkey is supposed to
have that mark on his back.

An old legend says that the donkey in the
Garden of Eden laughed when he saw the first
man, and God was so angry that he said the
donkey should always laugh whenever he opened
his mouth to make a noise. But, after a little
while, when the donkey was very sorry for what
he had done, God promised that one day the
little grey animal should have a chance to make
amends for his horrid laughter.

It was a long time before that chance came.

Then, one spring day, when crowds of people
were tramping and riding into the capital city
for the great feast, a donkey pulled at the rope

which tied him to his stall. He was near a cross-road, and able to see the passers-by, and he was still young enough to wish he could go with them and see what was happening. Suddenly he felt a man tugging at his bridle. Looking up, he saw two strange men who began to lead him away. At first he was very frightened, especially when they led him into the middle of a large crowd of peasants. Then he heard a voice which was gentler than any he knew. A hand was laid on his back, and a moment later a man was sitting on him, moving him forward towards the city. Not even the shouts and the waving branches and the clothes they threw down in the road in front of him frightened him while the man on his back patted his neck and calmed him.

You know who the man was on the donkey's back, and where they were going?

It was Jesus, riding the donkey into Jerusalem on the day we call Palm Sunday.

There are people who will tell you that ever since that day the donkey has had a cross on his back. It is the mark that shows he was once used by Jesus.

Another legend is told of the robin. Once, they say, he was a very ordinary little brown bird with an ordinary brown breast. But there came a day when he saw a man hanging on a cross. On his head was a crown of thorns, and one of the thorns was hurting the man's forehead, making it bleed.

The robin perched on the poor man's head and tugged and tugged at the thorn, until at last he managed to pull it away. In doing so his little brown breast was stained with blood.

Yes, it was Jesus whom the robin helped. And ever since that day the robin, they say, has had a red breast. Like the donkey, he has a mark which shows that he helped Jesus—and, in some way, that he belongs to Jesus.

Now I don't think either of those stories is quite true, though I'd like to think they were. But I'm sure of one thing. People who *do* belong to Jesus have something about them which shows other people that they are His. It won't be a mark on your body, like the donkey or the robin. But people will see, and know, just the same.

How do you think people can recognize that you are His?

Of course they were kind—and kindness is a great thing. The donkey wasn't hurt at all by his kindness—but the robin was, for a little thorn stuck into his own breast. To belong to Jesus is to *serve* Him, even if sometimes it isn't easy, even if we get hurt, or laughed at, for our loyalty.

Bear the
marks of the
Lord Jesus.

NERO IS ALIVE!

ONE of the very worst rulers of the Roman Empire was Nero. His family hated him, the ordinary people were frightened of him and the Christians thought of him as Antichrist— that is, one who was not only the opposite of everything that Jesus was, but one who would destroy all that Jesus stood for.

The Emperor knew that he was the most hated man in the Empire, and he knew that the only way he could remain on the throne was by keeping everyone in fear. He poisoned some of his own family; had those who were the people's favourites put to death; and had spies everywhere in case there was any talk of rebellion.

The Christians he treated worst of all. When Rome was burned down, about thirty years after Jesus' death, he spread a rumour that it was the Christians who had done it and then there followed a time of dreadful persecution for those who followed Christ. Christians were tortured, thrown to the lions in the Coliseum, covered with tar and burned as torches for the Emperor's games. Many who had no love for the Christians were horrified by these things.

Plots were laid in Rome, and in other parts of

the Empire, but most of them came to nothing. Then, at last, news reached Rome that one of the Roman generals in Spain, Galba, had called his soldiers to revolt against Nero. Word spread through the army, and the soldiers turned against the emperor they hated. Soon Nero realized that his days as emperor were ended. He fled from the city of Rome and took refuge in a villa not far away.

Even his own personal guards turned against him and very quickly it was known in Rome that he was hiding in the villa. There could be no escape. It would not be long before the soldiers, or the common people, found him and dragged him out to his death. In despair, Nero took the Roman soldier's way out. He killed himself, all alone in the house. When they found him, he was dead.

The Empire was filled with relief and joy. At last the tyrant was dead. There need be no more fear of torturing, poison or the lions. It was all over.

Or was it?

Nobody quite knew where the rumour started, but somewhere in the East men began to whisper that Nero wasn't dead, after all. He had come back to life—and, what is more, he was marching on Rome at the head of an army of fierce Scythians who had good reason for hating the Romans.

The rumour spread, faster and faster, through the bazaars of Syria, the little towns of Asia

Minor, until at last it reached Rome itself.
Villages were emptied as the peasants fled for
their lives. Shops were closed in the towns of
Asia Minor, and people planned where they
would go when Nero and his army approached.
In Rome, those who had led the rebellion
trembled with hopeless fear. Nero, they knew,
would have no mercy on those who had betrayed
him, or plotted against him, or run away.

There would be no mercy.

It was no more than a tale. Nero was as dead
as ever. He never came back.

But someone else did, thirty years or more
earlier.

Jesus came back.

How do you think people felt about *that*?

We sometimes imagine they were thrilled and
happy. Perhaps they were. But what about
Peter, who had denied with oaths and curses that
he had ever heard of Jesus? What about James
and Andrew and Matthew, who all ran away?
What about Thomas, who refused to believe it?
Or Caiaphas or Pilate who had sentenced him to
death? Don't you think that, at first, they must
have been just as frightened as the people of
Rome when they heard that Nero was alive?

What would Jesus do—if He really *was* alive—
to those who had deserted or plotted against
Him? Wouldn't He be furiously angry, and
make them suffer for what they had done? Most
people would have done so.

This is the really extraordinary part of the story. Not that Jesus came to life again, and showed Himself alive—but that He behaved as He did. It is just here, at the end of the Gospels, that we see what Jesus is like and what God is like. It is here, most of all, that we see what His love and His forgiveness mean.

"Jesus is alive!" they cried. "And," they added, "though we can scarcely believe it, He loves us still!"

Ascensiontide

MARY BROWN

MARY BROWN lived with her mother and father —and did just about as much work in the house as most of you do. Sometimes she made her bed before she went to school—and sometimes she didn't! Sometimes, when she couldn't get out of it, she washed up the tea-things or dried them and put them away. She never pretended she liked doing it very much, even if she *was* a Girl Guide.

Fortunately Mother never seemed to be ill and was always there to make the breakfast—though Mary could manage to scramble an egg if she had to. Dinner was always ready when Mary came home from school, and the house was always clean and tidy. There wasn't even much shopping left for the week-end, when Mary was home from school.

Not that Mary was lazy. She could always manage if she had to, she thought—and hoped she would never have to try.

But one Friday, when she came home from school, Mary found her Mother shivering and looking dreadfully ill. The tea was ready, though, and Mother wouldn't go to bed, whatever Mary said. When Father came home it was different. "Off to bed you go!" he said—and Mother went.

'We'll manage, won't we, Mary?" he said, as Mother went out of the room. Mary said "Yes" very firmly—and hoped that by the next day Mother would be better.

She wasn't. She was worse. There wasn't anything else for it. The doctor came and had a look at her and shook his head very solemnly. "At least three or four days in bed!" he said, and then looked at Mary. "You'll have to be Mother for the week-end," he told her, and left her with a prescription to be taken to the chemist straight away.

It wasn't only a note for the chemist that had to be taken, however. There were the things Mother had been too unwell to do the day before. There was the grocer and the greengrocer, and back to the greengrocer for what Mary couldn't carry the first time. In the middle the laundry came, and Mary had no sooner got back upstairs with the change than the bell rang again. This time it was the butcher's boy with the meat.

Mary took it upstairs to her Mother. "Whatever are we going to do with *this*?" she asked. "Shall I send it back?"

"Good gracious, no! You'll have to cook it to-morrow—though I expect Daddy will help!" said Mother with a smile. "Now, is the kitchen tidy?"

"Yes," answered Mary. "But I've still got to

wash up the breakfast things and dust the lounge.
I'll have a shot at lighting the fire after that."

Somehow, even with Daddy out at work, she
managed to get it all done. Perhaps it was a good
job, after all, that she had been a Girl Guide for
two years!

The next day, Sunday, there wasn't any church
in the morning either for Mary or Daddy.
There were potatoes to peel, vegetables to wash,
meat to cook, gravy to make and . . .

"Oh dear," said Mary, "we've forgotten the
pudding!"

"Well," answered Daddy, "we'd better do
what we've been doing all morning. Run up and
ask Mother what to do about it!"

Mary went. "Plums in one of the bottling
jars—and you can manage some custard, can't
you?"

"Yes," replied Mary. As she got to the door
she asked, "Do you make it with milk or water?"

Somehow they got through. Mary even got
through the next two days when she had to stay
at home from school to look after Mother. On
Tuesday night her Mother got up for a while, and
came downstairs to look round.

"So you've managed it—on your own!" she
smiled. "You see, you *can* do it, when you have
to!"

Mary smiled too. "Yes, I suppose that's true.
I can manage when I must. I can't always rely
on you. But, you see, the important thing was

that you were there all the time. I could always come and ask what to do and how to do it. It wasn't as though I was *really* on my own!"

Do you see why Jesus went away from His friends, the disciples? One reason, anyway?

They had to learn to manage on their own. While *He* was there they relied on Him to preach, to teach and heal, to lead them. When He went away, they managed. *They* preached and healed. *They* led the people, even in the worst times.

But there was one thing that mattered. Jesus was always there. They could always ask what to do and how to do it. Jesus always answered, even if sometimes in ways they hadn't thought of. They were not *really* on their own.

ascension day.

Whitsuntide

ANOTHER MAN'S MIND

THIS should really be a talk about the Holy Spirit, since it is Whitsuntide. Instead, we are going to talk about our minds.

What is your mind?

The part of you that thinks, I suppose is the best answer. When you can't help poking your nose into what somebody else is doing they are very likely to tell you to "mind your own business", which means think about your own business. And when you haven't "got your mind on your sums or your grammar" you can't do it because you are really thinking about something else.

There are times when you are stuck with a problem at school and you wish the teacher would come and lend a hand. When she does, you feel crosser than ever because all she says is: "Well, *think* about it. Work it out in your own mind. *I* can't do it for you." It's true, of course. She knows the answer and she knows how to do it, but *her* mind can't do your work for *you*.

Nobody can have someone else's mind, can they?

A great author, John Buchan, once wrote a story which you will read for yourselves. It is in a book of short stories called *The Runagates Club*. It is much too long to tell here, but I'll give you an idea

45

of what it is all about. We needn't use the names in the book—instead we'll call the two brothers, about whom the story is written, John and Tom.

They were both clever. People sometimes thought that Tom was even cleverer than John, but they liked John best. Somehow he seemed to find it easier to be good and to do the right thing. Perhaps Tom wasn't really bad, but he just hadn't the power inside him to do the right thing, especially if it was easier to do the wrong one. We have all felt like that at times.

As they grew older, they grew apart from each other. Those who knew them said: "We knew John would turn out to be the best of the two. Look at the work he puts in. See how he helps people. He'll be a Member of Parliament before he's finished, you see!"

Their friends would answer, rather sadly: "Yes. But think about poor old Tom. Just as clever as John—and see what a mess he's made of his life. Can't pull himself together. He'll never do much now. It's too late for him to change!"

Then a dreadful thing happened. There was an accident, and John, the good one, was killed. Can't you imagine people thinking: "What a pity it had to be John. It wouldn't have been nearly so bad if it had been the other one."

But now something queer seemed to be going on. It was as though Tom had suddenly pulled himself together. He stopped doing the bad things, quite suddenly. He seemed happier. His mind itself seemed to have changed. It was just as though he had determined to take his brother's place in the world—as though he was going to do all the things his brother would have done if he had not been killed.

You're quite right—he *did* do what his brother would have done, and he made an even better job of it. But no one could understand how it had all happened—and just from the moment when John had died. Perhaps Tom himself didn't really know either, although he had his own explanation.

"When my brother died," he said, "it was just as if, in that moment, when his mind was free of his body, that mind of his got into me. As though it took the place of *my* mind. As though I hadn't my own mind any longer. I couldn't even think as I used to think, and didn't want to do the things I used to do. It was as though John was living in me."

Now we ought to be talking about the Holy Spirit, oughtn't we, since it is Whitsuntide? In a way, we have been doing so. St. Paul says more than once to the friends to whom he wrote his letters something like this: "Let the mind of Christ live in you."

That is what the Holy Spirit does. He is, in a way, the mind of Jesus—who was always good and wanted to be and do good—living in us. If we let Him into our hearts then we do the things He wants done, and think the things He would think, because His mind is in us.

The Fellowship of the Holy Spirit, the mind of Christ.

Empire Day

THE SHIELD OF ACHIMOTA

HAVE you ever heard of Achimota? Do you know whether it is a man or a place? You will have heard of it before we have finished.

Or have you ever heard of Aggrey? He *was* a man—a real man and a great man. His full name is too much to remember, but his friends knew him as Kwegyir Aggrey. Do you think you can guess which country he came from?

He was born in Africa, on the Gold Coast, in 1875. He must have been as loveable as all African babies and as lively as all African boys. He went to the Mission school, where he learned what it meant to be a Christian, and where his teachers very soon found out that he was likely to make a name for himself. *They* thought he might make a name in his own district, or even in the Gold Coast as a whole. But they had no idea his name was going to be known all over Africa and America, and in most other parts of the world.

To be a teacher was the ambition of most clever boys who went to the Mission schools, and Aggrey followed the same line as the rest. Very soon, however, to the astonishment of many, even of his best friends, he left West Africa for America to learn more about the world and about

48

the subjects he was most interested in. There he became a professor in a Methodist University in North Carolina, and later in Columbia. He was preaching, teaching, speaking and writing all over the place, and Americans, Britishers and Africans realized that here was a great man— perhaps the great African of their own day.

Not that everybody liked him. There were plenty of people who despised him just because he *was* an African, just as folk to-day dislike Africans or Indians because their skins are a different colour from our own. He was often turned away from hotels because no dark-skinned people were allowed to stay there. He had to ride in the part of the trams or trains which were reserved for negroes. Even on ships crossing the Atlantic he was given a table where no one else sat, a cabin where no one else would sleep with him because of his skin.

You can imagine that treatment would make make most of us very bitter. It is one of the things that has made Africa a problem-country in our own time. We would probably say one of two things. Either, "If I were born again I would like to have a white skin and not a black one"; or, "If I had the chance I'd show these white men that they're not as big as they think they are!"

Aggrey was talking one day to someone who had asked him what he would say to God if he had the chance of being born again . . . would he want to come to the world next time as a white man? Aggrey answered: "I would say to God— 'Make me black, Lord. Make me as black as you can make me!'" He was more proud of being an African than anything else.

What about "getting his own back on the white men"?

After the First World War had ended in 1918 the Government decided to build a huge and important college in the Gold Coast at a place called Achimota. It was to have primary schools for boys and girls, secondary schools and so on. The Governor needed a Principal—a European, of course, in those days, and a great missionary was chosen. This missionary, Fraser, accepted the post as long as Aggrey was Vice-Principal. So Dr. Aggrey came back to his own country, to give the best of his life and his mind to training his own people.

A magnificent job he made of it, too. But don't you think that he must sometimes have said in his own mind: "One day, when we're educated and powerful, we'll push these Europeans out of our land"? We *know* he didn't think that—and we know because of the shield that he chose for the College.

It is a shield which shows the keys of the piano—eight white notes and three black ones. Just like the sharps and flats and white notes on your own piano at home. Aggrey chose that for a r eason that you can guess. "You can't play a go od tune on a piano just by using black notes or white ones. You need both. And to make a good world you need black and white, working and playing together."

At the back of a great biography of Aggrey is a map of the world and over Africa is printed a huge black question mark. We might in our day put a question mark over all the world. It can only be taken away when black and white, African and Asian and European and American, learn the meaning of the shield of Achimota.

Christian unity

— *Roman Catholics*
Anglicans
Methodists

— *sacrifical Tumer*

"Yonder lies the Enemy"

THE PROPHET AND THE FRUIT

A VERY long time ago there lived a shepherd, who spent part of his time caring for the fruit trees round his own house. He was a good, honest man, who found it possible to make a living in the open air. Like many of his own people, even though he was a countryman, he could read and write, but there were very few books in those days for anyone to read, and little time for it, too. For the most part the shepherd learned from nature. Like Jesus Himself, who lived hundreds of years later in the same country, he knew the world of animals and birds and men better even than the world of books.

He knew that the wind from the east might drive the locusts towards his trees. He knew the cry of a strayed lamb in danger, when a lion or a jackal was leaping on it. He knew that when the fruit came in the summer the end of the year was drawing near—harvest would come and go and the winter would be with them before they had realized it.

God was very real to him, out there in the open air. He disliked the towns, and thought of them as wicked places, as they very often were.

One day, however, something made it necessary for him to go to the king's town. It was crowded with gaily dressed people, all on holiday. The king himself was in the town, too. Amos— for that was the shepherd's name—disliked it all from the moment he stepped into its streets. He tried to get lodgings, but the prices that were being charged were wicked. Poor people couldn't possibly pay that much. Amos knew that he would have to sleep in the open air, and was glad to be under the stars again. Next day, as he wandered about the town, he saw that although the poor people looked gaily dressed, their clothes were really patched and ragged. Many of them were only there to beg for money—and the rich folk, in their good clothes and their jewellery, gave them very little.

In the market place Amos saw shoes for sale, and as he stood by a stall he heard someone saying: "Look at those shoes. What a price just for a pair of shoes! I could pay all my debts with that money if I had it!"

He went on to the temple and was horrified to find that all he had heard was true. This was not a temple to the God he worshipped. There were strange gods here, from other countries. He was so angry that he could hardly speak, especially when he heard that the king himself would soon be here to worship these strange and evil foreign gods.

And these Jewish people were the very people God had helped and saved, the nation that God

wanted to use in telling the world about Himself!
Amos walked slowly away from the gate. As he
did so, he saw a man sitting selling fruit. Summer
fruit, such as he was growing in his own orchards.
He asked the price, and couldn't believe the
answer. All that! For fruit that he could eat by
stretching out his hand on his own land.

Summer fruit, indeed! He found himself
saying it over and over again. *Kais!* That was
the word for it in his own Hebrew language.
There was another word like it. *Kes,* the word
that means "the end". He found people were
listening to him, and talked more loudly. "Look
at it," he said, "this summer fruit. You know that
when it comes the summer is here and the spring
is over. Soon it will be over, too. It will be the
end. Why, even the words sound alike. And,"
he went on more angrily, "*this* will be over too!
All this wickedness—this greed of rich people for
more money, this cruelty to the poor people like
you and me, this dreadful worship of strange
gods. Do you think God is going to let this go on
for ever? Of course He isn't! He will end it!
Something will happen to this king and his
nobles, and to the country we live in, too. You
wait and see. You won't have to wait long!"

As he spoke there was a shuffling amongst the
people and Amos looked up to see the priest of the
temple staring at him. But instead of stopping,
Amos only went on more angrily, and the crowd
grew bigger every minute.

Suddenly the priest spoke. "Get home, you silly shepherd," he said. "Go back to your sheep, your silly sheep, and your . . . your summer fruit! Nothing will happen to us. God doesn't notice us, even. But something will happen to *you* if you're not out of the town by the morning! You'll be put in prison and probably killed. Get away from here!"

Amos went. Not because he was a coward but because he had something to do. He went home to write down what he thought and believed. We have his book in our Bible. He was perhaps the first prophet to write his message for the people. The priest tried to stop him talking and set him writing instead—a much more useful way of spreading his message.

Amos was right. God does care about people and what they do.

ESCAPE FROM HOLINESS

A MINISTER asked one of his congregation who was back from holiday what the church was like in his holiday town. "I'm afraid I didn't go," said the man. "We went walking over the moors on Sunday. Did us no end of good. Much more than sitting in a crowded church!"

Do *you* go to church on holiday? Or Sunday-school?

Lots of people think holidays are a time for getting away from things like church. Even when you don't go away to the seaside or the country, you may be tempted to say: "Why should I go to church to-day—I'm on holiday, aren't I?"

Holidays surely haven't got anything to do with holiness!

There are three words which are all tied up together, even if they don't seem like it.

The first two are "holidays" and "holy-days". After all, there is only one letter different and you know enough about writing your own language to know that when you add another word to one ending in -y, you change the "y" into "i". So that "holidays" and "holydays" are really the same word.

That's not surprising. In olden times no one

56

thought of going away to the seaside for a holiday.
For one thing, travel was almost impossible.
For another, money was scarce and if you didn't
work you didn't get paid. It was work for most
ordinary people, from light until darkness, either
in the fields or in their own homes, spinning or
weaving or cobbling. The only times they gave
up working and feasted or danced were on the
"saints' days" or the great festivals of the
Christian year.

"Saints' days" or "festival days" are called . . .
what?

"Holy Days." The only breaks in the dull
routine of life, then, were "holy days". In time,
quite naturally, "holy days" became thought of
as "holidays". If it hadn't been for the Church,
people would have had very few holidays indeed.

Now for the third word. It sounds very much
like "holy"—can you think of it?

It is "whole".

When we say that something is "whole" we
mean that it is all there, that it has all its parts
complete. A "whole house" is one that is complete, not left half-finished. A "whole man" is
what? Arms, legs, head . . . yes, the things that
make a body. And something more than that,
for we are able to think as well as see and hear
and smell. A "whole man" has a mind as well
as a body. And more than this, too, for we have
a part of us which knows about God. Our souls.

A "whole man" has body, mind and soul—

and he must care for each part. A "whole man" living through a "whole day" will use his body, and exercise his mind by thinking, and allow his soul to feel alive by talking and listening to God.

If that is true of a "whole day" at any time of the year, it must be even more true of the "whole days" that we call "holidays"—even if we forget they are more truly "holy-days".

Holidays are meant to do three things, if they are whole holidays, and not just some kind of "half-holiday".

We shall make sure our bodies get the most out of this time of relaxation. We shall use them to the full, by walking or swimming or riding— and not just lazing about. Few boys and girls want to "sit about" on holidays, anyway.

We shall use our minds. We ought to know more about our own country, more about other people. More about how other countries live, perhaps, if we have been to the Continent for our holidays. We shall have a mind more richly stored if we use our holidays properly.

But this isn't the end. We started off by talking about going to church. That isn't the most important way of keeping a holiday "holy", though it helps. We will remember God as Creator, when we tramp across His good earth and sail across His blue seas. We will understand Him as Beauty when we see the loveliness of the flowers or forests or sunset sky. We will recall the "lastingness" of His promises when we see the snow-clad Alps or the great mountains of Wales or Scotland.

Everything in our holiday world—even people—has been made by God to tell us something more about Himself. When we understand this, holidays are turned into "holy-days" and we return from them more completely "whole people".

Harvest Thanksgiving
HARVEST SPELLING LESSON

THIS spelling lesson is really for the juniors, though the smaller ones who are just learning to read will be able to help us a lot.

Do you like spelling? What do you spell with?

Perhaps you use letters in school—but here we are going to spell with flowers and fruit and vegetables and other things as well.

First of all, in this spelling lesson, we need a "G". We could have something golden, or a gladiola. But, instead, we will have something that stands on the table. It hasn't any colour, and doesn't look very beautiful—but it is one thing we couldn't possibly do without. Water. And if you think that begins with a "W" we will have what is on the table—"G" for glass of water.

Now some fruit, for we must have some in the lesson. "O" for orange.

And a flower. Could you have thought of anything as lovely as this autumn flower if you were making a world for the first time? You know what it is called. Dahlia, with a "D".

There is our first word. GOD. And already we have thought of the way in which God has given us loveliness . . . refreshment . . . and something we couldn't do without.

The second word is a very small one.

First, an "I". Let us have something that people think is a weed—for God made them, too, and there is a use for most of them, as we are finding out. Here, on our Harvest Sunday, we use it for decoration. Ivy.

Only one more letter in this word. What do you think the word is? It might be "in" or "it", but it's "is"; so we need something beginning with "S". You can have your choice, for there are lots of things in a Harvest which begin with "S". What shall it be? Shallots, another vegetable. Or scabious, another flower. Sweet peas, very late ones. Or spinach?

Now we are beginning the third word. The first letter is . . . How many of the bright ones can guess what it is? Those who know their Bibles will do so.

"L". What shall it be? Probably nothing you are thinking of. This spelling lesson is made up of things which God created. When you look at all the lovely flowers and fruit at the front of the Church you can't help thinking how full of colour they are. But we might not see the colours at all if God hadn't created something else. What lets us see these shapes and colours? Eyes, certainly; but there is one part of the twenty-four hours when your eyes are not much use to you. The darkness—when everything is the same grey colour. So what do you think "L" had better stand for . . . one of God's greatest gifts to us? It is Light.

It is queer that at a Harvest we haven't mentioned anything about harvest. We can't go on like that. The next letter is "O". We had better make it something to do with the cornfields. "O" for Oats. Almost everyone in the world needs food made with corn—usually some kind of bread. We should be very badly off without it.

What do you think the next letter is? "V". Can you see anything beginning with that awkward letter? It would be a poor Harvest service that hadn't got some grapes somewhere. And grapes grow on . . . Vines. It is just as well to have that word in our spelling lesson, because Jesus taught us a great truth when He was once talking about grapes and vines. Do you remember the text? "I am the true vine, and you are the branches." How does it go on? "Unless you abide in me and I in you, you can do nothing." "You in me and I in you." Just as the grapes and the vine they grow on belong together, so God and ourselves belong together. We can't even live without God. Or without what He gives us. Think of the things we have mentioned. Some of them we *must* have—water, corn, light. Some help us grow strong bodies—fruit and vegetables. Some seem to have been given to us only because of their beauty. Other things, like weeds, people find uses for in time.

So the text is "God is Love". What should the "E" stand for? "Everything".

Or it might stand for "Even Me".

THE PALACE OF PEACE

Do you know what is the capital of Holland? In The Hague you'll find the Royal Palace and the Dutch Houses of Parliament. You'll see lovely shops and not far away is one of the splendid bathing beaches which no one outside Holland can pronounce—Scheveningen.

At Zorgvleit, one of the districts of The Hague, is another palace, with a tower which rises 260 feet above the ground. Round about it are delightful gardens and inside are magnificent rooms into which any visitor may go. A guide who speaks Dutch, German, French and English will take you round and show you all the sights.

No one has ever lived in the Palace—at least, no king or queen or president. Its name is the Palace of Peace—and a very queer business it all is.

In 1899 the first International Peace Conference was held in The Hague, and it was decided, first of all, that there should be no more wars, and secondly, that a building should be put up in The Hague where the nations could come together and talk over their problems instead of fighting about them.

A competition was held, for which architects

63

all over the world entered, to discover the best design and, soon after the new century had begun, the foundation stone of the Palace of Peace was laid. Six years later it was finished.

In this magnificent building, where the International Court of Justice now meets, there are some very lovely things—nearly all given by one country or another.

The entrance-gates were the gift of the German Government, and the wrought-iron gates and bronze doors of the vestibule came from Germany.

As you look along the outside of the building you find it is built on granite which came from Sweden; and granite from Norway was used for the porches.

In the vestibule you catch sight of a wonderful bronze and crystal candelabra hanging from the roof. The guide will tell you that it was given by the Austrian Government.

From the vestibule you enter the Great Hall, with corridors reaching away along the buildings, a sweeping staircase leading upwards to the big conference room and the Court of Justice, and through the windows a glimpse of an enclosed courtyard with a fountain playing in the centre. But you mustn't wander too far away or you won't hear the guide. He is telling you now that the tremendous vase you see here came from Russia—and it stands higher than you do yourself. There is another priceless vase from China, and others from Hungary.

On the walls are paintings, and some of the
rooms are hung with old tapestries. Both of these
things were the gift of France. The stained glass
in the windows of the Hall and on the staircase
was Britain's gift. When you climb the stairs you
see a huge group of statues, which travelled across
the Atlantic from America. The carpets you
walk on are almost priceless. Some were from
Rumania and others from Turkey. Holland
itself gave decorations for the walls, and the
fountain in the courtyard, with polar bears
standing at each corner, shows that Denmark was
"in" at the beginning of the Palace.

Do you know when it was finished and opened?
In August, 1913.

And do you know what happened less than a
year afterwards, in August, 1914? The first
Great World War began.

Germany, which gave the entrance gates,
marched into Belgium, which had given the
doors. Britain and France, forgetting their
windows and their paintings, sent their armies to
fight against Germany. The lights in the vestibule
didn't mean very much to Austria then. She
stood beside the Germans in the trenches in the
war which went on for four long years. The
countries which had built the Palace of Peace
were at each other's throats.

Why? Because the nations which had built the
Palace had spent very little on peace itself. A
vase or a carpet may be valuable to a collector,

C

but it would not cost a country very much of its annual revenue to make a present of it to the great building in the Hague. Peace costs more than that. It costs time, and thought, and energy. It costs pride and service and understanding. It cannot be gained for the price of a fountain or a stained-glass window.

All Saints' Day

THE SAINTS OF ROME

THIS is the time when we remember "all the saints".

At once some of us think of stained-glass windows in cathedrals and parish churches, or of the legends of St. George and the Dragon, and of other saints whose crosses we have in the Union Jack. Others will think of St. Peter and St. John and then St. Paul, the saints of the New Testament. They all seem a very long way off from ordinary people like ourselves, don't they?

Do you know that Paul once wrote a long letter to people who were becoming saints? They lived in Rome and were really the first Christian Church in that great capital. We know the names of several of them, because Paul sends special messages to them at the end of his letter. But I don't think any of them imagined that they were saints, even if Paul gave them that name at the very beginning of his letter.

There weren't any churches, as we know them, in those days. Christians met to worship in private houses, and a good deal that went on in these houses was open for those outside to see and hear. There were probably several houses in Rome when Paul was alive where the Christians met together. We know who owned two of them, at any rate.

One belonged to a Roman officer called Pudio and his wife Claudia, and there are men who believe that this man Pudio was the general who came to our own country, and ruled over the southern half of Britain. In those days he was a worshipper of the Roman gods, and built temples to them in Chichester. But after he returned to Rome he became a Christian and opened his home for his friends to use as a place of worship.

How he was converted no one quite knows, but it is said that his mother was a friend of two of Paul's best friends, Priscilla and Aquila. If so, he might very easily have met them and come to know of Jesus through them. Certainly *they* opened their own home to the Christians. Under the arches they went on with their work of making and sewing tents during the day-time, and talked to any of their customers who would listen about Jesus and His ministry. Paul's name must very often have been mentioned, for Paul himself had lived with them for a long time, and worked at the tents with them, too.

What about the Christians who came to their house?

Some were Jews, who were working in Rome.

Some were business men, important in the workaday life of the great capital. We know this because the lady who brought the letter from Paul to Rome was in need of help from such men and Paul tells them to help her in any way they can.

Others belonged to the Emperor's palace itself. That doesn't mean they were what used to be called courtiers. There are clerks and cooks and grooms and scores of other folk who work at our own royal palaces in London and Windsor. Many of these Roman Christians would have been doing the same kind of work for the Roman Emperor. One of them was called Stachus.

Then there were servants and relatives of some of the great men of Rome. Narcissus himself had been put to death by Nero, and Aristobulus, the grandson of Herod the Great, was a Jew who lived in Rome instead of Palestine, and died there, too. Neither of them were Christians, but their houses were kept up after their death by their families, and some of them belonged to the Christian church which met in Priscilla's house.

Women were there, as well as men, even though women had very little to do in those days except look after their homes and their husbands and children. There were Mary and Tryphena and Tryphosa, for instance. Queer names, but real women.

Slaves, too—for Urban, Hermes, Hermas, Julia and Philologon, are all common slave names.

It's a queer mixture, isn't it? Soldiers and tent-makers, generals and slaves, men and women, Jews and Romans and Greeks . . . all making up the church in Rome.

They don't sound much like "Saints", do they?

But a "saint" is somebody who is *being made holy*, not someone who *is* holy, and still less someone who thinks he is! That is what the Church is for . . . to help to make us holy, more like Jesus, day by day and year by year. The Church has always been made up of ordinary people . . . but because we belong to the Church and, more important, because we belong to Jesus there should be something different about us. Something that reminds people of Jesus—and brings other people into the Church and to Him.

THE LAUBACH WAY

THIS is St. Andrew's Day—but we are going to talk about someone much more modern. He is an American of the twentieth century, while St. Andrew was a Palestinian who lived almost two thousand years ago. You will see, however, that they both share the same idea —and it is one of the most important ideas in the world.

Do you know that probably about three-quarters of all the people in the world can't read? Can't read, that is, in their own language. Indeed, many of the languages which people speak in Africa, for instance, have never yet been written down at all. They haven't even got an alphabet.

Think of some of the things you cannot do if you cannot read. If you live in a town, like many Chinese or Indian folk, you can't read the names over the shops, or the place that is written on the front of the tram or the bus, or add up the bill which the man in the shop gives you. You can't write a letter, however important your news may be—and it may very well be that if a letter comes to your village there is no one living there who can read it. You have got to pay someone to read it and pay him extra to write the answer.

71

Certainly you couldn't read the newspaper or a book. And if you were an African from the bush, for instance, and heard for the first time the stories of Jesus, it would be no use your buying a New Testament or a Gospel, because the little black signs which we know as letters would mean nothing at all to you.

Dr. Frank Laubach is an American who is changing all this.

How long does it take someone to learn to read in your school? A year, or two years, perhaps, before we can read well. Or even longer.

You can't imagine fathers and mothers, and even grannies and grandpas, coming to school to sit with boys and girls and learn, can you? It would be much too long a business for them even to begin.

Dr. Laubach has found a way of teaching people to read more quickly than you learn even in your own schools, sometimes. We needn't worry much about how he does it. That is another story, which one day you ought to be told. It is done by charts, with letters and pictures. But even if we don't go into all that, we can still see what happens when the teacher comes to a village where no one can read.

First there may be a story—and the book is shown to them from which the story comes. "How would you like to make these little black marks tell you the story themselves?" The older folk don't believe it is possible, but some of the brighter young people, and the boys and girls, are interested. A little group is picked out. Then comes the first chart. Pictures of things they can recognize—a man, a tree, a banana, an elephant. Then they find they are making sounds, and the sounds all have their own mark— we should call them "letters"—on the paper. In an hour they have finished their lesson and they must go home to practise it.

The next morning they are all back again, with eyes shining. They can read the lesson!

"Can we learn some more to-day?" they ask eagerly.

Here comes the bad moment. "No!" They all begin to talk at once "Why not?" "Don't we know it well enough?" "*I* can do it—listen to me, teacher!"

But the teacher says the same thing to all of them. "You must prove that you know it by teaching someone else to read what you have learned. *Each one must teach one more!*"

Think how fast people could learn to read if they all did that! "Each one teach one!" The Indian Government has said that it could make sure that every one in India could read in twenty years by that method.

But where does St. Andrew come in?

Well, it was St. Andrew's method, too. I don't know whether he was much good at preaching, especially to crowds of people. But do you remember what he did when he first met Jesus?

Look it up in the first chapter of John's Gospel. He went off straight away and brought *one man* to Jesus—his own brother Simon Peter. Or, do you remember what he did when there was a crowd of hungry people? He didn't try to organize a big scheme. He brought one boy to Jesus. *And Jesus used the ones he brought.*

What is the best way to fill the church, or get boys or girls to club or Sunday-school? The Laubach way—St. Andrew's way.

Let each one bring one.

Overseas Missions

THE PRAYER THAT WORKED

You sometimes hear preachers, especially
missionaries, say in a missionary sermon:
"There's one thing you can do to help the Church
overseas. You can pray for it." Very often we
may have thought: "What's the good of that?
Prayer can't really *do* much!"

This is the story of a prayer that did something.

Samuel Rahator was an Indian minister. His
story is full of excitement, and one day, when
we are talking about real people, you ought to
hear it. This is only just a little bit of it.

Rahator had not begun life as a Christian, but
when he was a young man he had been converted
and, after carrying on with his own work for a
while, be became a preacher and then a minister.
At first he worked in Bombay, but after a while
his Church decided that they wanted him to try
and do something about a district near Poona,
where there were very few Christians, and where
Christian people were bitterly persecuted.

Up-country Rahator found life very different
from Bombay. He lived in a small Indian town,
and toured the villages, teaching and preaching
about Jesus. Often he found people were willing
to listen, and here and there little groups of

Christians grew up who built churches or schools. Other evangelists joined Rahator in his work.

There was one place, however, where things were very hard indeed. True, there were a few Christians—just two or three families. Whenever he came to the town—it was called Akola—Rahator heard stories of how badly these people were treated by their Hindu neighbours. They were persecuted. They were not allowed to sing their hymns and say their prayers aloud. They could not build a prayer-hut, since all the land belonged to the Hindu farmers. These Hindu folk were frightened that if they let Christian people live and worship in their village their own gods would be angry and perhaps send plagues or illness to punish them.

Nothing Rahator could do seemed to stop their persecutions.

At last he made up his mind that there was only one thing to be done. He would make one last journey to Akola, and one last appeal to the elders of the village. If nothing good came of it, he would not waste time going again, but would advise the few Christians living there to move to another place where life would be easier. It seemed like cowardice, and yet it was the only sensible way.

Along the Akola road Rahator made his way. When he reached the place he found the village council were already meeting together and he asked to speak to them.

He found them looking solemn and angry. Nothing he could say would move them to a kinder attitude. They would not allow Christians to build a prayer-house, nor to worship or sing or pray where anyone could hear them. Indeed, they didn't want them in the village at all.

Sorrowfully Rahator gathered his little Christian group around him and led them out into the jungle. There, they spent an hour praying and afterwards sadly said farewell to each other. Rahator promised to try and find somewhere else for them to live. Then he left, to make his way home.

After he had gone about a mile he heard someone running and shouting his name. It was a messenger from the village elders. He was to return at once as they wanted to see him.

Wondering what new mischief they had in mind he faced the elders once more. When the leader spoke he could not believe his ears.

"Padre Sahib, we have changed our mind. If you will send a teacher to Akola, we will build him a house and a school, and allow the Christian people time and land to build a prayer-house of their own."

Rahator went home wondering if he had heard aright, and then wondering why this incredible thing had happened.

Later, he found out.

Rahator was a Methodist, and the Methodist Church, for many years, has published a little book called *The Prayer Manual*. In this book, the missionary districts of the Church are divided amongst the days of the month, and in each district the urgent things are set down for people to pray about. When he reached home Rahator picked up his Bible, his hymn-book and his Prayer Manual. As he opened it, he knew the answer to his question.

That day, members of his own Methodist Church all over Britain and in the missionary districts were praying for *him*.

Medical Missions

ONE PAIR OF HANDS

IN the western part of India is a large Indian town, where very few Europeans live. In the centre of the town a large Hindu temple, with its great carved gateway, towers over the houses. There are always dozens of people moving in and out of it, and on great occasions the pilgrims come in hundreds and thousands. Many of them are ill, with old sores on their bodies or eyes which are diseased. Beggars sit about the square and when you look at them you feel that it is very likely they are suffering from leprosy. The priests in the temple don't much care about healing sickness, as long as the pilgrims worship the old gods, and bring their money and their gifts.

There *is* a hospital in the town, and in it the nurses and doctors are always busy. The wards are crowded with patients and their friends and in the rooms to which the "out-patients" come there are long queues.

Three miles outside is another hospital.

This was built by one of the Missionary Societies. Here, too, there are very few Europeans. The nurses are almost all Indians and so are a couple of the doctors. Every day the out-patients' department is full, and there is always a big queue still waiting for attention when the doctor closes it down for the day.

Inside, the wards are crowded. Not all those who come can be given beds, and although they are willing enough to lie on the floor, there are not enough nurses and doctors to care for all who want to come.

One day the nurse who was looking after the out-patients came out from the doctor's surgery.

"No more to-day," she told them.

At once everyone began to say how ill he felt, and how likely the baby was to die before the morning. She held up her hand.

"No more medicine, and no more time. The doctor has to go through the hospital now." Then she looked at their sad faces.

"Go back to the town," she told them, "and try the Government hospital. They may have beds there if you are ill; and their doctors may have more time than we have to-day."

The people began to shuffle away.

"Why do you come all this way?" she asked, as they went. "You have to pass the town, and walk three miles beyond it to get here. What makes you come, when you can just as easily stop at the hospital in the town?"

There was a little silence before one old woman answered.

"We come to you, nurse, because *your hands are different!*"

Isn't that a grand thing to say about people because they are Christian? The medicines are the same, and the beds are just as hard in the Christian hospital—but Christians' hands have love in them.

Some of the Hindus in this town believe that their gods came into the world, as Jesus came into it. But they all think that the gods became men to enjoy life. If there was any question of suffering they went away again. Christian people believe that Jesus shared all the things that people suffer—and the Gospels are full of stories of His love and His healing.

Jesus doesn't go about the world healing folk now, but He told his friends to do what He had done. One of His commands was: "Go and heal the sick." That is why Christian hands ought to be different—they belong to Jesus, and we know that *His* hands would have been gentle.

In some countries mothers and fathers never worry very much about girls being sick, though they would be very worried if the boys were ill. They can't understand why Christian nurses take as much care over girls as boys.

In India, where the hospital is that we have been talking about, people who had the dreadful disease of leprosy were just pushed out of the village to live or die in the jungle, away from everyone else. No one could understand why the Christian Church started hospitals for poor people who suffered from leprosy. "Those people have been cursed by the gods," they said; "why should anyone worry about them?"

But *we* know why. Medical missions are the best way of preaching about a God who loves men and women. They let us show, through hands of love, that God cares for those whom nobody else ever wants to help.

WHO DOESN'T KNOW THAT?

HAVE you ever been in a house where a little boy has gone to school in his first term and come home very excited because he has found out that the earth is round or three times three make nine? And then the big sister of seven suddenly looks down her nose, and says: "Who doesn't know that, silly?"

There are things that *everybody* knows. Like Christmas being Jesus' birthday; or that stealing is wrong; or that you shouldn't talk in church.

But I wonder if everyone *does* know them?

Of course people in Africa or India may not know, but surely everyone in our country does. That's why we send missionaries to countries which aren't Christian, isn't it? To tell them the good things we know about God, who is our Father, and Jesus, who came into our world.

Can you say the Lord's Prayer?

A hundred boys were being taken into the Army, not long after they had left school. They gave their names in, and got their khaki clothes. They found where they were to sleep and eat. The doctor saw them, and their officers, and then the padre came. You know what the padre is, don't you?

He found that out of those hundred English boys there were more than thirty who couldn't say the Lord's Prayer, even when they were helped with the beginning. They had never learned it—though they were supposed to have known it at school.

A man was sitting in a bus in a big city a few days before Christmas. The shops were brightly-lit and the windows were crowded with lovely things—toys, clothes, presents in Christmas wrapping paper. Across the market-place stood a tall Christmas-tree, with fairy-lights in its branches. At the bottom stood a box with masses of parcels in it—toys which people were giving for poor boys and girls.

As the bus went across the square they saw that the tree was standing just in front of a church, on the steps. People were going in and out of the open church doors. A lady sitting by the man on the bus suddenly said: "Why do they have to mix Christmas up with the Church? What's it got to do with the Church, anyway? It's nothing to do with religion!"

The man was sure she was joking at first, but the woman was quite serious. So he asked her if she knew why we had Christmas. She didn't. He asked her if she knew it was Jesus' birthday. She didn't know that either. So he asked her if she had ever heard of Jesus Christ at all. Oh yes, she said, she had heard the words. They were bad words, and she wouldn't ever let *her* children say them!

That is a true story—and so is this.

There was a Youth Club in a town in the North of England, and lots of the boys and girls who came to it had never been to the church's Sunday-school. One day the minister asked some of the club members to come to church for a special Youth Service. They said they might come, but they weren't sure. On the Sunday evening about a dozen of them *did* come.

They sat at the back and the boys kept their hats on until someone came and asked them to take them off. They said they never did in the pictures, so why should they—but they did. They talked very loudly before the service began. One of the girls powdered her nose and another boy passed a packet of cigarettes round, but at that moment the minister came into the pulpit and the boys put their cigarettes behind their ears. They behaved dreadfully during the service until the sermon. Then they listened— partly because it was short and partly because the minister really talked to *them*.

When it was over they gave him a good clap!

They were dreadfully upset when someone said: "Sh! You mustn't clap in church!" "Why not?" they said; "we always do in the pictures!"

Do you know none of them had ever been

inside a church before? They didn't know how to behave because they didn't know why people went to church or what it was for!

Missionaries for Africa and China! Yes, and missionaries for Britain, too! Lots and lots of boys and girls and men and women don't know anything about God or Jesus or the Church, even in our own country.

And we've got to do something about it.

HORSESHOES AND FAGGOTS

You know what rent is? And we usually pay it in money. It is the amount we pay for the place we live in, or work in, to the person who owns it. Don't forget that, because we shall need it again before we have finished.

Rent is not always paid in money.

The queerest rent in England is paid in horse-shoes and horse-shoe nails, in hatchets and bill-hooks. It is paid in London with great solemnity. And it is paid to the Queen! What is more, this particular rent has been paid in this way for seven hundred years.

It is true that the Queen herself won't come and collect it, but the man who does it for her will be dressed in legal robes, wearing a full wig such as judges wear, and will receive it in a court-room with some of the officials of the City of London in attendance to make sure everything is done properly.

More than seven centuries ago, a piece of land was given to the Corporation of London. It was known as "The Moors" and was somewhere in Shropshire. The rent had to be paid to the King—and it consisted of two knives, one of which was blunt and the other sharp. In time the knives were changed to a bill-hook and a hatchet, though nobody knows why. In time, too, the Corporation of London, many miles away, forgot about the land, so that now no one knows where it was. But the rent is still paid, and each year the Queen's Representative comes to collect it.

The Solicitor of the City of London produces a bill-hook and a small hatchet, and a little bundle of faggots. He chops up the faggots into small pieces with the two implements, to prove that they are sharp, and then hands them over. The rent for the land that can't be found has been paid.

Before this happens, however, the other rent is paid—and we *do* know why this is done.

The part of the City of London which is now known as the Temple used to belong to the Knights Templars. A good deal of it was used for tournaments, especially a field called "The Thickets". In 1135 a knight called Walter le Brun (you know what that means) was engaged in a tournament and needed his horse shoeing. A smith, who had a forge in the field to repair the knights' armour, was called to do the work. As a reward he was given permission to build a forge in one corner and keep it there permanently. (I should think Walter le Brun must have won his tournament!) For this privilege he had to pay a certain rent each year . . . not in money, but in horseshoes and nails.

How the field came into the possession of the

Corporation of London no one knows, but as the years passed the rent was paid to the Queen or the King, first by the smith's descendants and then by those who owned the land later on, that is, the City of London.

So, each year, when the Queen's Remembrancer, as he is called, comes to collect his bill-hook and hatchet, he is also presented with a number of gigantic horseshoes. They are too big for most modern horses, but would be just the thing for one of the great Flemish mares used in the mediaeval tournaments. With the horseshoes are sixty-one nails, used to fasten them to the horses' feet.

It seems a queer custom to be going on in the twentieth century, just as it did seven centuries ago. The reason it does continue is not just for the sake of keeping up a tradition, but because kings and queens and people in important places believe you should pay for what you possess, if it really belongs to someone else.

You have got to pay your rent.

There is a movement for men called Toc H— we shall hear about it another time—which thinks one of the most important things anyone can do is to give service to other people. Not just kindness, but kindness that costs something. Service is being helpful to other people when you could be doing something for yourself. It is the Scout's good turn. Or the club member doing a job of work instead of just playing games. Or the

Church officers spending time looking after Church property, or the Church's money; or young people teaching in Sunday-school or working as Guide or Cub officers. Or the members of your local Council doing their job; or the women who do voluntary nursing or reading to old folk or caring for little children. The important thing about it is not just doing the job, but doing that instead of doing something just for yourself.

If you ask: "Why should we, anyway?" there is a good answer.

Toc H, which I mentioned, has a definition of service.

"Service," they say, "is the rent we pay for our room on earth."

Temperance Sunday

KHAMA THE FIGHTER

HAVE you ever heard of the Bamangwato? They are a tribe of Africans who have been a good deal in the news, and for many years they had the greatest and best chief in South Africa as their leader. His name was Khama, which means "The Antelope". It had been given to him because he was so fast a runner that he could keep pace with a galloping horse.

The first part of the story happened when he was only a young prince, not chief of all his people.

Khama was out with the warriors of his tribe. The fire glowed on their shining skins. They looked great warriors—but in their eyes there was fear. The boasting that they made was not matched by their actions. They were hunting a lion which had ravaged their flocks for many weeks. Oxen and cows had been killed. Everyone was terrified. The hunters could not catch the lion, however much they boasted; though they were always talking of what they would do when they and the lion came face to face.

The fire burned brightly and one by one the hunters went to sleep, except the six-foot young man who stood leaning on his rifle. When they were all sleeping he slipped away. Not until the morning came did he return. Over his shoulders hung the skin and the mane of a full-grown lion. Khama had killed him, alone, while the hunters slept.

Khama was the hero of the tribe, and as the years went by he became much more greatly loved than his wicked old father, Sekhome. The old chief plotted against him and tried many times to have him killed, for Khama had become a Christian while Sekhome his father remained a witch-doctor. He refused to marry more than one wife, to have anything to do with the heathen practices of his people, or to deal with the witch-doctors. They knew well enough that if Khama lived their power would go.

One night Sekhome did his worst. He gathered all the witch-doctors of the tribe together and Khama wakened to hear the sound of their chanting. He had been brought up to be terrified of these men's power. Their charms were supposed to bring plague, blindness, madness and death. As Khama listened he knew that his old father was making the biggest magic of his life—and it was against Khama himself. He was to die, in agony, as a result of their spells.

Khama must have felt afraid. Anyone would have done, watching the bright flames in the darkness and seeing all the witch-doctors in their fiercest clothes, dancing round the fire. But, whatever he felt inside, Khama left his hut and walked towards the circle. He pushed the men on one side, with their lions' claws and horns rattling round their necks, looked for a moment at the fire, with charms burning brightly. Then he walked into the fire and stamped it out with his bare feet. The witch-doctors fled into the night.

But Khama's biggest fight was still to come.

When he became chief he knew that his people were free from the fear of wild animals, of witch-doctors and of their enemies. But there was a worse foe still. While Khama was defeating his enemies—the Matabele people—his young brother, as wicked as his father had been, was encouraging the Bamangwato people to brew beer and get drunk.

Khama, coming home again from the wars, knew that beer and spirits would do more harm to his people than anything he had already conquered. Men and women were already lying drunken in the shadow of their huts. There was only one thing to do—drive out his young brother, who put temptation in the tribespeople's way, and get rid of those who would not do without drink.

"I will not have drink in this town," he ordered.

Then came the white traders, bringing crates of beer with them. But Khama's answer to them was the same as to his own people. "If you want drink you may have it—but not in my town."

It was his worst fight. It meant standing as an African against the white men who believed they were the lords of Africa. But Khama won his fight. And until he died, an old man of ninety, he kept his people free from the evil that threatened to break down their manhood.

He must be a hero to every man and woman who wants to keep mind and body clean.

Education Sunday

HOW DO YOU LIKE YOUR TEACHER?

THIS is Education Sunday, so perhaps we had better talk about school!

And you can look as miserable as you like about it! If there weren't any schools you would be a good deal *more* miserable! Perhaps you are always ready for holidays at the end of the school term, and you think it would be nice if somehow you didn't have to go back again when the holidays are over. But you know very well that there was a time when hardly any children went to school in England and those who had no school to go to didn't have holidays, either.

You can remember some of the things they had to do . . . working down in the mines, pulling the trucks where there were no ponies; climbing up chimneys to sweep them; doing heavy work in factories to which their mothers and fathers had sold them because they had too many children to feed at home.

It wasn't really much of a life when there were no schools to go to. Even where children did go to school, it wasn't as happy a place as yours is.

Have you ever heard of Squeers? He was a schoolmaster in a novel by Charles Dickens. The book was called . . . ? *Nicholas Nickleby*.

Nicholas went to Mr. Wackford Squeers' school as a teacher—fortunately for him he didn't have to try and learn anything! The school was called Dotheboys Hall—and it didn't do the boys any good, either. Mr. Squeers mixed up working and spelling. Like this:—

"Spell window, boy!"

The boy looked terrified and said nothing.

"Window! *Window!!* w . . i . . n—win; d . . e . . r—der! Winder—window. Now go and clean it!!"

And along came Mr. Squeers with his stick in case they didn't!

Not much of a school-master, was he?

There are three kinds of teachers.

The first one sits at his desk and says: "Now I'm going to tell you how to do long division" (or something of the kind). "You put down the figure you've got to divide. Put it down. 176598. Now, you've got to divide 15 into that. Listen very carefully. Put 15 under the 17. Take it away. Remainder 2. Bring down the 6. 26. 15 into 26, 1 and 11 over. Put the 1 at the top and bring down the 5. 15 into 115 . . . ! Can you understand what I mean?"

I hope you say "No", and say it very loudly. Because *I* wouldn't be able to understand if he just sat at his desk and told me what to do. I should want to say . . . well, what would *you* want to say?

"Will you *show* us how to do it, please?"

The second kind of teacher does show you. He puts it all down carefully on the blackboard, and every now and again he turns round and asks: "Do you see how I'm doing it?" When you see him doing it in front of you, it seems easy enough. Until you try it for yourself. Then, somehow, although it was easy when he did it on the board, you still get stuck. Perhaps the teacher is back at the desk now, taking no notice. He's told you how to do it and you must get on with it. What do you want him to do?

Come and help you. Certainly. And the best kind of teacher won't do it all for you, but he will be there, ready to come along and bend over your desk, and help you when you are stuck. With his help, it comes out right.

There was a man who called Jesus a teacher. Do you know who it was? Nicodemus. What kind of teacher is Jesus?

He tells us what to do—how to live, that is. He tells us to be honest, and helpful, and useful; never to lose our tempers, always to be forgiving; to pray, and to remember that God is always near us.

If He simply told us how to live it would seem so hard that we should think no one could ever live like that at all. So He lived in our world, the same world which we live in, and He showed us how that kind of life can be lived. His disciples watched Him, and tried to be the same. But they were not any better than we sometimes are.

D

But Jesus, you see, was the best kind of teacher. He didn't only show them how to live—He was there to help them to live the right kind of life. Just as He is always at our side to help us.

Industrial Sunday

MORSE

THERE are people who think that God made a very fine world which was made up of trees and flowers, animals, birds and men, skies and seas . . . and that afterwards men "took over" and got on with the job of making the world interesting and easy to live in.

Well, the first part is right enough, but not the second. God *did* make the world we live in. He made men's bodies—and their minds. He made them able to think and work. It is no use any of us imagining that we would have thought out the clever things we have done—the cinema, television, radio—unless God Himself had given us the kind of minds we have.

Whatever would we do without telegrams? Some people are a bit frightened when they see the telegraph boy coming up the garden path with a little yellow envelope, though usually it isn't bad news at all. But a great deal of the business of the world is carried on by telegraph. Just think of some of the things you can do with it.

If you are on holiday with your aunt at the other end of England, and she wants you to stay an extra week, you can send a telegram home to your mother and ask her. It might be easier than asking her on the telephone! If somebody is getting married, you can send them a telegram and wish them luck. If your father has a birthday and he is away from home you can send *him* a telegram. Somebody in Scotland can send flowers by telegram to a friend in London . . . the flowers don't exactly come down the wire from Scotland, of course! A business man in South Africa can order something from another business man in America or Britain in the same way. And, of course, it is cheaper than talking to someone at the other end of the world, or the other side of the world, on the phone.

We should be in a dreadful mess if something happened to all the telegraph wires in the world and all the cable lines under the sea.

One of the greatest men who had anything to do with all this was a man called Samuel Morse. Have you ever heard his name?

Well, you've certainly heard of the Morse code. All dots and dashes. It is by that code that messages go all over the world across the telegraph and cable lines.

Samuel Morse was a young American who wanted to be an artist. He came to England in 1811, when he was twenty, to study art in London, and a very interesting time he had there. As he crossed the Atlantic, he thought what a wonderful thing it would be if only there were some kind of lines under the ocean by which messages could

go from Britain to America and back. But the
very idea seemed too silly for words. Fancy
having a line which stretched all those thousands
of miles! (That, of course, was about a century
before wireless was invented.) You couldn't
even send messages from one part of the town to
the other!

All the time he was working at his painting and
his sculpture, Morse was thinking about electricity,
too. In 1832 he was travelling from France to the
United States with a Dr. Jackson, who knew a
good deal about electricity. They talked about
it, and drew plans on little bits of paper, all
through the voyage. When it was over Morse
still went on thinking.

He gained no money from his ideas, and for a
long time lived in poverty, for there was no money
in his painting, either. But twelve years after that
voyage across the Atlantic something happened
which was going to change many people's lives.
Morse had worked out a way of sending a
message from one place to another, along electric
wires, just by tapping out a lot of dots and
dashes. You know enough about the Morse
alphabet to know that three short taps or dots
means "S", and three long ones means "O" . . .
and then another three short ones is another "S".
Every sailor knows that "S.O.S." signal.

It was in 1844 that the first message was sent in
this way by telegraph from Washington to
Baltimore. Since that day almost every country

in the world has taken up Samuel Morse's idea of telegraphing messages. What a brilliant man he was to have thought all that out so long ago. What a brain he must have had. And what courage to go on, in poverty, while everyone he talked to laughed at his ideas. But that wasn't what Morse thought about himself and his invention.

The first message that was ever sent, on that day in 1844, was this:

"What hath God wrought!"

Church Anniversary
ADMIRALTY ORDERS

In the West of England there was once a village built near the cliffs. Indeed, it was so near that many people who drove through it felt that it was dangerous. Not that the people who lived there minded very much, since they had lived there all their lives and were used to it. But it was very exposed, too, and in time, as some of the old stone-built cottages grew more and more broken down, newcomers, and young people who got married, instead of going into the little cottages near the cliffs, moved about a mile inland.

Their homes were more sheltered, and more modern, too. The old people who had never lived anywhere else declared they couldn't live out of sight of the sea, but they grew less and less. Other folk felt that those in the shelter of the valley were sensible, and as time passed more and more houses were put up in the new village, and fewer and fewer remained on the cliffs.

Those which were there fell into ruin. Their owners didn't see any reason for repairing homes that no one now wanted to live in. At last there was nobody left in the village on the cliffs at all.

Travellers saw sheep wandering amongst the ruins, and straying where the gardens used to be. Children would point to the rabbits which popped in and out of the burrows they had made amongst the tumble-down houses. Flowers which had once been cultivated now grew wild, and the only person who ever stayed in the old village was an occasional tramp.

The only building left of any size at all was the old church. Its tower, set high on the cliffs, could be seen far inland, and every ship passing up or down the coast could notice it easily. But what was the good of a church building in a village where no one lived?

The answer was easy. No use at all.

The pews were taken out, and their wood used to make new pews in the new village church inland. The windows were removed—at least what was left of them after boys had been throwing stones. A hole appeared in the roof and grew bigger as the rain ran through and the wind blew the slates away.

Nobody cared. Nobody wanted the old church.

Then one day a letter came to the vicar. It was followed very soon by a visitor.

The stranger came from London, and when the vicar had asked him into his study they began to talk. They talked of the days when the village used to be on the cliffs; of the way folk had moved away; of how the houses had fallen down since nobody needed them.

"The old church is falling into ruins, too," said the vicar.

"Exactly. That's why I've come from London to see you. I've been sent by the Admiralty— you know, the department which looks after ships and sailors and so on. When are you going to repair the church?"

"Repair it?" asked the vicar. "We're not going to repair it at all. Nobody wants that church now."

"Indeed they do," said the man from London. "*We* want that church."

"Why ever should *you* be interested in it?"

"Because that church is marked on all our charts—the charts the ships carry up and down the coasts. No matter whether they're little fishing vessels or big liners, they have that church marked on their charts." He looked at the vicar. "They need the church to steer by." He got up from his chair, looking very serious. "We need the church. And if you can't repair it by yourselves we must give you some money to do it with. But don't forget. We can't do without it!"

A great many people need the Church for that reason—your church . . . all the churches together . . . God's Church. If the churches all fell down, or were closed . . . if there were no services in church or on the radio . . . if there were no Sunday-schools for children to learn the right way to live . . . then we should have very little indeed to "steer by". Very little to tell us the right way to go or the right thing to do.

Don't let anybody ever persuade you that you do not need the Church.

Family Service or Parents' Day
FESTIVAL OF LIGHTS

CHURCHES overseas often make use of festivals or tunes or architecture which belong to the country. It is no use expecting someone who has always been used to singing in an Indian fashion to start singing our chants or hymns. And they may very well ask: "Why should we give up all our old customs when we become Christians?"

One of the loveliest of all Indian festivals is called *Divāli*. On that night every Hindu house is lit up with little lamps, set in rows on the windows and roofs, and a village, for once, looks like fairyland. But with this festival there goes idol-worship and gambling in which no Christian could possibly take part. So the Christian Church has taken over some of the custom and added a new meaning to it.

Imagine, then, that you are in an Indian village. It is evening, and the stars are beginning to twinkle in the dark sky. Many of the villagers are Hindus, but everybody is interested in what everyone else does. On this night, some of the Hindus are clustered round the little Christian church at one end of the village. Others are standing in the doorways of their huts, or under the palm-trees by the village well, watching what is happening. It is easy enough to see into the church, for the windows are wide open on this warm autumn night.

Inside the church, the men are sitting on one side and the women on the other, as they always do. Children sit everywhere, or run from one side to the other occasionally. The only light in the building is a small lamp which stands on the Communion Table.

As the service comes towards its end, the village pastor stands by the table and calls out the elders of the families. Mostly those who get up from the floor and come out to the front are men—fathers and grandfathers—but there are some women, widows mostly. They stand in a line before the pastor, looking very solemn. Each one holds a little saucer lamp in his hand, unlit.

The pastor asks the congregation to stand, and then tells the family elders to repeat three sentences after him.

The first is: "Jesus Christ is the Light of the World."

They all repeat it together. Then the other two follow.

"Jesus Christ is the Light of my Life."

"Jesus Christ is the Light of my Home."

Then, each elder steps forward and lights his lamp from the one which stands on the Communion Table.

After another hymn and the blessing, the elders go back into the congregation. Each one collects the members of his own family round him and leads them out of the church into the village compound. As they walk across to their own homes the little lights of the lamps flicker in the darkness.

All the non-Christians watch them.

They watch them afterwards, too.

This service is the beginning of the Christian Home Week. During the days which follow a service is probably held in each Christian house. Old pictures are taken down, and new religious ones, probably very cheap, are put up on the walls. But these are only the outward signs of being Christians. The family begins to hold family prayers, if they have stopped during the past year. They read the Bible together, and since Indian houses in the villages are not very large they often do these things outside, where everyone can see—and hear.

So other people have a chance of hearing the Christian good news.

But the Hindus will be asking questions which have nothing to do with singing hymns or reading the Bible.

"These people," they say, "have said that Jesus Christ is the Light of their homes. Very well. Reading the Bible and saying their prayers is part of it. But what are they *really* like at home? Are they good-tempered or bad-tempered? Do they keep cheerful when things go wrong? Are they helpful to other folk as well as themselves? Do they ever say or do things which they would be ashamed for us, or for Jesus, to know about?

"Is Jesus Christ *really* the Light of their lives and their homes?"

It is a question we can all ask ourselves.

Sometimes to be a Christian at home is the most important thing of all—and it is certainly not the easiest place, unless Jesus really *is* in our hearts.

THE CAMERA

THERE was a little gathering to say farewell to a man who had worked for many years in the headquarters of one of the great Missionary Societies. He had written books which had been best-sellers on missionary affairs; travel books which were full of colour. He had travelled in Europe and Africa, China, India and the West Indies. For a very long time he had been Editor of one of the best-known missionary magazines. To all these occupations he had given one splendid talent.

He was one of the best photographers in the country. His missionary books and travel books gained readers because they were so beautifully illustrated. The missionary magazine which he edited had some of the best pictures of all religious journalism. Wherever he went, his camera went with him. Long after he retired, and probably even after his death, his photographs would provide a history of missionary activity, a record of primitive life and village customs, an illustration of the Church's activity which would be immensely valuable.

At that little farewell gathering the Editor told

a story which he had never told or written before.
It was a tale about himself.

When he was sixteen, he said, his father asked
him what he would like for his birthday. He
knew very well what his answer would be. A
camera! On his birthday, the present was put
in his hand.

"If you want a camera," said his father,
"you shall have a good one. This is the best
that can be bought. It should last you all your
life!"

The camera began to work that very day, and
for weeks afterwards it was kept busy. There
were photographs of his family to be taken.
Then of his friends, and of places to which he
went. It was clear at once that he had a talent
for the business.

One Sunday night he went to church as usual.
Perhaps he wasn't going to attend very carefully
to the sermon, but the preacher took an odd
text.

The story was the familiar one of Moses and
the burning bush. You remember how he was
acting as shepherd for his father-in-law, and how
his attention was drawn by a bush about which
there seemed to be a strange flame. That wasn't
the really important thing. What was important
was that God Himself spoke clearly to Moses out
there in the open air. He thought, as he had so
often thought, about his own Jewish people in
slavery in Egypt. He thought again that some-

body should do something about them; somebody should lead them out of their slavery into their old homeland. But who?

God's voice came clearly. "*You* are the man!"

Moses rebelled at once. He was wanted in Egypt for murder. He was not a trained speaker. He had nothing to give him authority, either with his own people or with the Egyptian Pharaoh. Nothing at all.

The God spoke again. "What is that in thine hand?"

"My rod," answered the shepherd.

"We will use your rod," came God's reply.

Whether the boy in the family pew listened to the rest of the sermon we don't know. The preacher went on to say that whatever you have in your hand, God can use it. That is why you have it. There is nothing, no skill or talent or ability, that God cannot use.

He ended his sermon by asking again the question he had taken for his text.

"What is that in thine hand?"

Deaville Walker answered the question. Almost aloud he said: "My camera, Lord!"

From that moment the camera was God's camera. It didn't mean that he never took photographs for fun. Of course he did. But several things happened. He saw his skill with it as a gift from God. He determined to master his camera completely; to be the best photographer it was possible to be; to use it, whenever it seemed possible, to help God's work. That was why he came to the Missionary Society in the end—and no one who knew his work, or saw his photos, or read his books or his magazine, had any doubt that the thing in his hand was God's camera.

What is there in *your* hand?

First avowal
intent like a
Pilgrim.

Children's Day

THE LETTER IN THE CROCODILE

(*For an occasion when we are thinking of the work of Children's Homes.*)

Do you like writing letters? Not even "thank-you" letters after holidays or presents? Well, they have got to be done; and in the end they have got to be sent, even if there are a good many mistakes because we have been thinking of something else while we have been doing them.

We might take more care over them if we thought somebody was going to read them, with our own name at the bottom, in a hundred, or a thousand, years' time. You don't often come across letters a thousand years old, do you? But there are some letters which are older even than that. You might even see some of them for yourselves one day.

About the end of last century archaeologists—do you know what they are?—were working in Egypt. They were digging up temples and tombs and other buildings which had been covered by the sand for hundreds of years. Two of them, Dr. Grenfell and Dr. Hunt, had been digging out a tomb with very great care. You never knew what you might find. There might be mummies of kings, or chests of treasure, for Egyptians buried their kings with treasure round them. Or there might be nothing, for other men—desert robbers—might have broken into the tomb long centuries before and stolen all that could be carried away. So the two men watched carefully while their workmen chipped away at the entrance door, and when the stones began to fall they moved them gently away. At last the tomb was open. Inside it looked very dark. You would have thought it was too creepy to go inside.

In they went—and what do you think they found? Crocodiles! Nothing but crocodiles. The old Egyptians thought they were gods, and just as they turned kings and queens into mummies, which remained through the centuries, so they preserved the old crocodile-gods. Here was a tomb full of them. They had been dead for fifteen hundred years. Slowly the explorers looked round, hardly believing their eyes. No treasure at all—only crocodiles!

One of the workmen suddenly lost his temper at so much wasted work, and flung his pick at one of the animals. The skin cracked, and out tumbled piles and piles of . . . not treasure, but letters. The old Egyptians had stuffed the crocodile skins with letters to help them to keep their shape, just as men stuff the animals in a museum to-day. Yet they *were* treasure, those letters, for every one of them had been written not so very long after Jesus and Peter and Paul had lived. There were enough of them, when they were copied out, to fill two large books.

There were letters about all kinds of things—and it will be interesting one day to talk about them. To-day I want to read you just one of them. It was written to someone called "Alis" by her husband who was in Alexandria. This is what it said:

"We are still in Alexandria . . . don't worry even if I stay on in Alexandria. . . . As soon as ever I get some wages I will send you something. . . . If you have a baby—good luck to you!—if it is a boy, let it alone. If it is a girl, throw it away!"

Yes, it really says that. "If it's a girl, throw it away!"

You see, in those days, throughout the Roman Empire, when a baby was born, it was brought to the father and laid at his feet. If he wanted to keep it, he picked it up. If he didn't he left it where it was. Usually fathers wanted the boys, because they would grow up and earn money; but they seldom wanted girls. You had to pay somebody to marry them.

If he left the baby lying at his feet, it would be picked up—probably by the mother—and taken away in the darkness. She would put it down in a public place where it would very quickly be seen as soon as the daylight came.

There were many people who made their

living by going round and finding babies like this. They would look after them, though not very well, until they were old enough to be sold as slaves. Amongst the papers that were discovered in Egypt when the crocodile was broken open are a great many which deal with this business of throwing babies away, and finding them to keep for slaves. It was a paying affair, and those who did it made plenty of money out of it.

Can you imagine *your* father saying when a baby girl has been born: "A girl! Take her and put her down at the bottom of the road! Somebody will find her. If they don't it won't matter. She'll only die."

You know why all this was changed, don't you?

It stopped because Jesus said that little children were as important to God as grown-up men and women. It stopped because Christian people just couldn't allow such things to happen.

Don't believe people who say Christianity hasn't done anything for the world. Tell them about the letter in the crocodile.

— H. D.

Decision Day

INDIAN GIFT DAY

SOME churches have bazaars to raise money;
others have concerts or garden parties.
Most of them, some time or another, have a
Gift Day.

You know how it works. The minister sits in
his vestry, or even outside the church, waiting for
people to bring him what money they can afford.
At the end of the day, it is usually surprising to
find how much money has been raised.

I wonder what would happen if someone came
and said: "I'm sorry I haven't any money, but
here are a dozen eggs." Or if someone else said:
"I've brought a pound of tomatoes and two
pounds of onions instead." The minister might
feel a bit like saying: "Really, you know, this
isn't a harvest festival . . . it's a Gift Day."

But there are plenty of places in the world
where a Gift Day seems like that—all mixed up
with Harvest Festivals. India is one of those
countries.

A missionary had once to hold a gift day in a
country village. There wasn't any church there.
In fact the people hadn't long been Christians.
For a long time they had worshipped the ugly
stone idol which "lived" in the little white-

washed temple outside the village, by the well. It was a horrible-looking creature, with four arms; and the old priest who looked after it was just as frightened as the villagers themselves of what the goddess might do.

When the first Christian preacher came to the village they stoned him and drove him away. He came back later, and talked to them again. Once more they drove him out of the village, and went and put more flowers in front of the goddess in case she was angry with them for even letting him inside the village. Then, one evening, just when the women were beginning to cook the men's meal, an Indian girl came to their huts. She had a white *sari* with a red border, and they might have guessed straight away what she was. Under her arm she carried a little box, with a red cross painted on it. What do you think she was— and what had she in the box?

She was a nurse from a Christian hospital, who was trying to find another way to the villagers' hearts. She didn't do any preaching, but she used a good deal of ointment on the children's sore eyes, and bound up a good many running sores. When she left they ran after her, asking her to come again soon.

"And please bring some more stories with you!" called the children.

She had been telling them stories of a great Healer, who loved men and women, and boys and girls. Yes, Jesus, of course.

Somehow they listened to her more easily than to the preacher. They learned the songs she taught them, and got to know the stories. After a few visits they told her that they couldn't understand why she should come to them time after time in this way. What made her do it?

Then she began to tell them more about Jesus, of His love for her and for them, and of how He had come into the villages to show men what God was like.

It took them a long time to realize that God was not like the ugly idol, harsh and cruel, but kind and loving. But at last some of them came to know Jesus in their own hearts. How they loved Him! He had done so much for them, freeing them from fear and giving them health. They decided that they must build a church where they could worship Him, and a house where a teacher could live so that he could teach others, too.

So here they were, bringing their gifts. They had no money. Instead they brought fruit, vegetables, a chicken or a goat . . . things which could be sold for money in the market. With the money the church would be built.

The missionary sat all morning and all evening, receiving their gifts. It was hot and he was very tired by the end of it, and he was just putting all the things together when an old man came along with a little bag.

"It is rice, padre sahib," he told him.

"How much is there here?"

"I do not know. I saved a little from every meal for weeks to bring to-day. Jesus has done so much for me and my family that I had to bring what I could."

"And you don't know how much is here?"

"No."

"You haven't measured it?" asked the missionary.

"Sir," answered the old man. "How can I measure what I give to God?"

Choir Sunday

THE GOLDEN VOICE

CAN you sing?
   I suppose everyone can sing a bit, though perhaps when you begin, at home or at school, other people don't think very much of it. They may call you a crow, rather than a song-thrush or a nightingale. I wouldn't worry about that, as long as you are singing because you are happy. You may be doing a better job with your singing than somebody with a much better voice than yours. What I mean is . . .

But let's have the story—and you will see what I mean.

It is an old story, and I think it was once told in a poem by a lady whose name I can't remember.

There used to live, high up in the French Alps, a number of men who wished to get away from the towns and cities. They wanted time to worship, and to think about God; though they spent plenty of time working as well. They lived in a monastery which was very near a road which led over one of the passes. During the summer, tourists passed by the monastery, but in the late autumn and early spring, as well as the winter, the road was often blocked with snow.

It was during the autumn, when the first snow-storms were sweeping the hills, that the monks looked out for travellers who were lost or in difficulties. They would go out, after a blizzard, with their big St. Bernard dogs, to make sure that no one was in danger. Sometimes, though not often, they were able to pick up a traveller and bring him to the warmth of the monastery, and keep him there until he was well enough to go on his way.

In the first great blizzard of one autumn the roads were covered with deep drifts of snow. It was snowing too thickly for them to go out and risk being lost themselves, even with the dogs, and they were wondering whether anyone might be in danger, when there was a faint ringing at the bell by the gate. At once two of them went swiftly to the door and opened it. Outside, collapsed in the snow, lay a man.

They picked him up and carried him into their warmest room. They removed his cold wet clothes, wrapped him in blankets and tried to revive him. After a little while he opened his eyes. At first he could not remember where he was or how he had reached such a place, but when he saw the brown clothes of the monks he recalled ringing the bell at the gate.

The stranger did not seem able to talk very much. He had been fighting his way through the snow for so long that he was terribly weak, and after he had had some soup by the fire, they put him to bed in a tiny room, where there was no more than a bed, a chair, a table and some pictures from the New Testament.

He lay there quietly, half asleep, and out of the darkness came the sound of voices, singing. He was so sleepy that he thought they might be angels—but he soon realized they were nothing of the kind. Angels would sing better than that! It was the monks in their monastery chapel, singing at the last service of the day. And what cracked old voices they had, too! Dreadful!

The next day they kept him in bed, and he heard them singing half a dozen times during the day. The singing was still in his ears when he fell asleep. The following day he was better. He moved about the monastery during the day-time and in the evening went to the chapel with the old men. After a little while he began to sing.

As he sang those nearest to him stopped. They couldn't help it. They had never heard such a voice. Soon they had all stopped. It was the most wonderful voice they had ever heard, and as he sang they knew how awful their own voices must sound. They felt they would never dare to sing their hymns again, after they had heard them sung like that.

The stranger ought to have been able to sing, for he was a great opera singer from Italy. He knew they were listening, and sang all the better for it.

But that night, as the old "Father" of the

monastery was going to sleep, he seemed to see a sudden light in his little room. Out of the light a voice spoke.

"I have been sent by God to ask why there was no singing in the chapel to-night."

"But . . . but," stammered the old man ". . . there was more wonderful singing than we have ever heard. A stranger . . ."

"We heard no singing in heaven," said the angel, and at once the light was gone.

Gift Day

SIMON'S RED ENGINE

As most gift services are held at Christmas, this is a Christmas story.

And, as they usually appeal most to the smaller children, it is a tale for the little ones.

Simon was six.

One Sunday afternoon his Sunday-school teacher told them all that the following week there would be a gift service.

"What's a gift service?" asked Simon.

"Well, first of all there will be a Christmas tree in the church. The service is going to be in the church next week."

"Will there be presents on it?"

"There will be presents if you put them there. That's what a gift service is. You see, you're not going to *get* the presents; you're going to bring them."

"Well, if they're not for us, who are they for? You?"

"No," said the teacher. "Not for anybody here. Tell me, did you have a lot of presents last year?"

"Oo, yes," said Simon, and began to try and remember all the things he had had in his stocking, and from his mummy and daddy, and from the postman in the parcels that kept on coming.

"Do you know there are lots and lots of boys and girls who hardly have any presents at all?"

"I s'pose there must be," answered Simon. "Children with no mummies and daddies."

"Poor children," suggested someone else.

"Yes. And the presents you bring next week are going to be given to children who won't have as much as you have. Will you bring some of your toys for them?"

"Yes," replied Simon. "I will. I'll bring lots and lots."

When he went home he told his mother straight away. After that he went to his toy-box and began pulling his toys out, until his mother told him it was tea-time.

"I'll give them a ball," he told her. "I've got four of them and two won't bounce. I'll take those."

"Oh, Simon. You can't take something that's no good!"

But Simon wasn't put off by that. Mummies were like that. On Monday he took out the toys his mother had put back. There were a teddy bear, a red engine, seven dinkies, the four balls, a tennis racket, a pistol. . . . He put them all out on the floor. After a while he picked up the red engine, and took it into the kitchen to his mother.

"Shan't give this one. I like it best of everything I've got. I'll give my dinkies. I don't want them, anyway."

"All right. But do you think you'd like to get just something that somebody didn't want?"

Every day Simon took his toys out and looked at them, and every day he changed his mind. On Friday, he took his red engine to bed with him and tucked it under the sheet.

"Shan't take anything on Sunday," he decided. "I like them all too much."

The next day, when the postman brought the Christmas cards, Simon looked through them to see if there were any that said "Simon" on the envelope. There was just one—a very big one.

"Open it, quick," he told his mother. Then he changed his mind. "No, let me do it. It *is* mine!"

The card was a real Christmas one. There was a manger, with Joseph standing by it, and Mary with the baby Jesus in her arms. But instead of shepherds and wise men there were little boys and girls. All of them had toys, and they were bringing them to Jesus, the baby. One girl had a teddy bear, another had a doll, and a little boy had a little red engine.

Simon looked at it for a long time.

"If I could take my toys to Jesus, I *would* give *Him* some." Then he looked very sad. "But I can't, can I?"

He said nothing about the gift service all day, though he played with all his toys. He didn't say

E

anything about it next morning either, but at lunch time he was very busy wrapping something up in a Christmas paper. He wouldn't even tell his mother what it was.

"It's a s'prise!" he said.

The parcel went to church with Simon, and he was the very first to go up and give it to his teacher for the Christmas tree.

Can you guess what it was? Yes, a little red engine.

"And I expec'," said Simon, "that Jesus is just as pleased that I gave it for the other children as if I'd given it to *Him*."

I think so, too. Don't you?

THE WOMEN IN THE WINDOW

Towering above Liverpool, when you look at it from the river, stands the Cathedral, still unfinished. It has some beautiful things within it and none are more striking than the windows which were presented in 1910. They were given by the Diocesan Friendly Societies—societies of women and girls. It oughtn't to be difficult to guess the kind of people the windows commemorate.

Set in the stained glass of these modern windows are the heads of women—not characters from the Bible, or saints from the Middle Ages, but women of modern days.

No Sunday-school could get on without its girls' classes; no Scout troop is really complete without a Guide company in the same church; no home can do very well without Mother. And no church can work without women. When God made the world he made it so that about half the people would be men and about half would be women—and, so far as we can see, no other arrangement would have worked.

Have you heard of Grace Darling? What did she do? Didn't she save men and women from drowning by rowing out in a dreadful storm to a wreck off the Northumberland coast? She is in these windows, the youngest face of them all, to remind us that God has given women the great gift of courage.

And Mary Ann Rogers . . . nobody may know her name now, but there was a day when everyone in Britain knew it because of the way she died. She was a stewardess on a Channel steamer who took off her own lifebelt to give to a frightened woman after the steamer had been wrecked—and refused to get into the full lifeboat herself in case she made it sink. That was the same kind of courage as Grace Darling showed.

There are women here who went overseas as missionaries. You may not know *their* names, either. Louisa Stewart, a missionary's wife who was killed in China at the end of the last century. Women have been martyrs, just as men have been, even in our times. Mother Cecile, who founded schools in South Africa and led other women to serve the African people. Anna Hinderer, another missionary in West Africa.

But not all who are in the windows were women like them. Some never went far from home, and two did their work in Liverpool. It would be best to tell their stories in full one day. One is Kitty Wilkinson, the woman who opened the first public bath-houses, who looked after orphans and received a splendid gift from the Lady Mayoress, though she chose to help other people by living all her life in the slums. She *must* have a story to herself some time. Another was Agnes Jones, who was only thirty-five when she died, and did more for Liverpool in three years than thousands of people have done in a whole lifetime. She was a nurse, who came to help in the Liverpool workhouse-hospitals. Can you imagine a hospital to-day where the floors are cleaned by dirty charwomen, who get almost no money and spend what they have getting drunk? Or can you imagine a hospital where the only nurses are patients who aren't quite as sick as those who are in bed? No wonder people died! And, since they had no relatives who wanted them, anyway, nobody cared how they died. Agnes Jones was asked to nurse in one of those hospitals and try to do something about them. She did! In the three years before she was taken ill herself and died she had completely changed the workhouse-hospitals, begun a proper system of nursing, cleaned up the wards, got rid of the drunken old women and made the City of Liverpool see how scandalous it was not to care for old, unwanted people.

In the window, too, is Alice Marval. *She* is one of the "real people" who must have a story to herself in another book. Like Agnes Jones, she did her work for only three years—in the city of Cawnpore, in North India. She, too, was a nurse and she died of plague. The whole city was full of it. A hundred people were dying every day of it. But Alice just kept on, sometimes in the little hospital and more often by the roadside.

Just before she died she saw some respectable men standing on the other side of the road, doing nothing—but looking.

These women are remembered in the Cathedral windows because they didn't just look. They were on the side where the work was done.

Other Talks to Children

LIGHTHOUSES AND OTHER TALKS
TO CHILDREN

by John Wilding

A collection of talks to children drawn from widely varying subject range.

6s. net

THE SURGEON'S SPEAR
AND OTHER CHILDREN'S SERMONS

by R. W. Stewart

These children's talks range in subject from the Ancient Trade Guilds and the Red Cross to the Armoury and the Tower of London.

5s. net